Get to Know Your Neighbor
By
Jessica Ward

Hi,

My name is Jessica. I want to thank you for purchasing this book. I hope to create a series of books for your enjoyment. So sit back, relax, and let me entertain you.

Jessica

Chapter One

It was 8:00 am, and time for Kathy to rise and shine. She has a few stops to make before she gets to Jean-Luc's house. Jean-Luc has been her friend since... well, since forever. They grew up together. His father owns a very well-to do day spa, while her father owns a prestigious financial corporation. Kids in school used to make fun of them and call them the "Silver Spoons," because of their wealth. Jean-Luc and her have been friends ever since. At 23, Kathy wants for nothing. Her dad sends her an allowance, so work is not a problem.

Jean-Luc is away on holiday for a month, and so she agreed to go and check his on his house every so often. It was good to have a friend that was a guy, who you could trust. He never tried to take advantage of her; always like the brother she never had.

Kathy, got up out of bed, and padded across the carpeted floor to the shower. She pulled back the shower door to turn on the hot and cold water jets to the shower. Kathy stepped into the marble tiled shower, and let the warm water flow along the length of her curvaceous body.

She took the bar of soap and lathered it up in her hands. She smoothed the soap onto her body, caressing the lather to her frame. First her face, then her arms, and underarms. She rinsed, and then proceeded to take the soap, but this time she worked the soap all over her ample breasts. She soaped up one breast, lovingly, lingering... taking time to give her breast the attention that she wanted it to have. She then repeated the same ritual to her right breast. When they were both lathered up, with her fingertips, Kathy massaged the soap all over her breasts. Finally, she worked her way to her puckering nipples. She loved to play with her tits. Circle after circle with her hands and fingertips she played with the lather of the soap on her titties. She felt a hot yearning building up inside. She playfully rinsed off her breasts, now turning her attention down her frame further.

Kathy soaped up her abdomen with the bar of soap, going further and further down the length of her body. She shuddered at how good touching herself was. She loved her body, and loved making it happy. Now, she worked the bar of soap down further... lower and lower, until she reached her shaved mound.

As much as she liked pussy play, she had to restrain herself. At this point, all she wanted to do was shove her fingers in her wet hole and bring herself off... No... She wanted to savor this... Make herself want this....

She lathered up her hand, and gently rubbed the pouting mound over and over again. Her breath quickening, she continued on smoothing, and smoothing the soap over herself. Finally, she began to finger her hot, wet, wanting slit. Taking her finger, and tracing her wet hole back and forth... Back and forth... Over and over again....

Kathy began to hear the wet sounds out of her creamy pussy. But one finger wasn't enough... Her greedy, wet cunt wanted more... So, she inserted another finger, that traced a wet path up and down her slit.... Back and forth... Back and forth.....

Finally, Kathy could bear it no more... Her breath quickening, her hips rocking to and fro... She finally shoved the rest of her fingers in her wet, wanting hole. She had to come... It was driving her crazy... She needed release... Her pent up desire could no longer be contained. She rubbed her fingers over her pulsating clit feverishly. The orgasm was so intense, that she cried out, "AHHH!," "Ohh!!!"

When she was satisfied, she finished her shower, shut off the water jets, and climbed out. She dried herself off, brushed her teeth, and padded out onto the soft carpeted bedroom.

Now, what to wear... It was a warm day, and so she wore a pink halter top, and a denim mini skirt, with sandals. She was about to get dressed as her naked reflection caught her eye. Her blue eyes caught her sexy titties, as well as her shapely form. Of course there was always her shaved pussy, that always demanded attention.

She looked at the clock, and it was only 8:45. She eyed her tits in the mirror. They were still hard. She swabbed her slit to find it still wet. She had the time....

Kathy reached in her drawer and took out her pink vibrator. She felt so deliciously naught, and free... She laid down on the bed, and turned on the vibrator. She loved to hear the humming of the vibrator. She caressed her titties with the vibrator. She loved it when her titties were hard. Finally, she put the vibrator down to start rubbing them herself. She rubbed them, then she would roll her tits between her fingers and her thumbs. Then she squeezed her titties with her fingers as hard as she could.

By now, her wet, steaming, creamy pussy could take being ignored no longer. Kathy took the pink vibrator in her hands, turned it on the highest setting, and ran it back over her slit over and over again.

With one hand on the vibrator, she took her other hand and lifted her hot hood. Kathy took the pulsing vibrator and ran it over her engorged clit. The orgasm was so intense that she screamed almost instantly. Over and over again, waves of pleasure, sweet painful pleasure exploded from her.

Finally sated she lie on the bed for what seemed forever. Then she got up, went back into the bathroom to clean herself up. She finally got dressed, and headed out the door. By that time it was 9:30 am.

Chapter Two

Cynthia lived across the street in a very prominent apartment building. At 28 she lived alone, no pets, no boyfriend, a very quiet lady. She was an administrative assistant for a company that sold metals. Finally, she took a day off because if she didn't, she would lose the time. She actually liked her routine, and almost felt bad at not being at work.

The day was warm and sunny, and so she had her tea out on the veranda. She was sipping her Earl Grey tea when she happened to look across the street.

"Oh my God! Am I seeing what I think I'm seeing? Is that woman really...?" Cynthia shockingly asked herself. Now this wasn't the first time that Cynthia had seen this woman across the street having relations with herself or someone else. She remembered when she saw the woman having relations with a man. She remembered some of the sexual acts that she had witnessed. Ashamedly, she remembered how she looked on, wanting to turn away, yet to mesmerized to quit looking. Just the memory made her feel warm and flushed all over. She remembered the man suckling the woman's breasts; him spanking the woman as if she were a naughty child. She remembered how red the woman's bottom was, let alone when he mounted her. Cynthia began to feel a strange warmth over her. Then watching the woman touching herself, in that way....

"Cynthia Jean!," she scolded herself. *"What is wrong with you looking at that filth, and that woman behaving like a trollop? You were brought up better than that!"* Immediately, Cynthia picked up her tea and copy of Wallstreet Times, and headed into the living room. *"This has just got to stop!,"* Cynthia said aloud. *"No one should have to witness such.... such... such... lewd behavior!,"* she thought.

But realistically, what could she do?

She then decided to write the woman a note and slip it under her door. While feeling a bit cowardly, at the same time, the other woman needed to know how offensive her behavior is, and that others do not want to view this public spectacle!

She sat down at her Queen Anne desk, and began to pen her note to this woman:

Dear Madam,
Perhaps you are not aware, but you please need to draw your curtains when
entertaining gentleman, or at least wear a robe, as opposed to romping around
without clothes on. It is becoming to be a nuisance, and I have no wish to involve
the police. Most well brought up people refrain from your way of life.

Kindly, do be more considerate!
A Concerned Neighbor

There... That pretty much solves it... I will deliver it today under her door.

Shocking... Just Shocking...

Cynthia draped her cardigan sweater over her shoulders, and proceeded to take the note, put it in an envelope to deliver it across the street. When she went to the lobby of her building, she saw Jared, a doorman, looking at a young girl with a very short skirt on.

"Hello Miss Cynthia," Jared greeted her. "That's Miss Wentworth to you, Jared." Cynthia flailed. "Perhaps instead of ogling that young woman, although scantily dressed, you ought to pay more attention to who comes and who goes." "Yes, ma'am," Jared sheepishly replied. *"God that lady is a bitch! Just like an old biddy. Can't even imagine trying to lay her. Probably would have a big list of dos and don'ts. You'd need an instruction manual to nail that! " Jared thought.*

With brisk determined stride, Cynthia strode across the street. She knew that the woman lived on the 5th floor. As the elevator opened up, out walked the offensive person that the note was intended for. Cynthia stepped back into the mailroom, and watched the person move past the doorman.

"Good morning Ms. Dexter."
"Good morning, Alex. How are you?," asked Kathy
" Fine ma'am. How about yourself?" asked Alex.
"Couldn't be better." replied Kathy.

*"Good Lord,"*thought Cynthia, *"Fraternizing with the help! What's next with this woman?"*

Cynthia then went to the mailboxes looking for the last name of Dexter. There it is... 525. She proceeded to go up in the elevator to the fifth floor. There she exited the elevator and began to look for 525. At last she came to the door. She then slid the note under the door, and left.

Chapter Three

Brad was working a half day today. He worked for a merchant card processing company. He was meeting a client at 2:00, and had the morning to himself. After his appointment he was going to meet Marcey for dinner at Chez Elle. He went out onto the balcony to enjoy the morning view. He started to think about things. At 26 his career was going well... He really liked Marcey... He had a great apartment in the city... All was well. What a beautiful morning...

Just as he was about to turn away, his eye caught something. He couldn't believe what he was seeing. He closed his eyes to open them to find he was not dreaming. He saw a naked woman on her bed....

She had something.... Oh my God... She has a vibrator.... She's rubbing it all over her titties... Yeah baby, make them nice and hard for ol' Brad. What's this.... Holy shit, she's actually squeezing her tits! She must be really horny. Looks like she's going to squeeze them off!! At this point Brad started to notice a bulge in his pants. Where was Marcey when he needed her? Hey, what's she doing now? She's putting the vibrator in that pussy of hers. Yeah baby... run it back and forth. Not too fast... Pace yourself... Brad wants to watch... Yeah... Nice and slow... Hey, you're going to fast... Holy Hell!!! I can see her clit and the vibrator rubbing on it! Yeah baby... Come for me... Come for the ol Bradster. Look at her scream! She must really need it bad...

Finally the woman finished, and he didn't want to be standing there, so he went into the apartment. He was hard. He went to the couch, and unzipped his pants. He laid back on the nice leather couch, and began to stroke his hard cock back and forth. *He kept imagining the woman touching herself, playing with the vibrator. He began to imagine himself with the woman... sucking her tits, eating and licking her wet creamy pussy. He wondered what she would smell and taste like. Making her scream and tear at the sheets... screaming and rolling from side to side... Then after she came, she would give him a good tongue bath.... That's right... She'd be all over his cock... licking it up and down.... Up and down.... The pressure building, and building, finally having her pretty red lips going up and down his cock. She'd suck him for everything it was worth. He'd get so hard, she have a hard time keeping him in her mouth. Her mouth would make slurping sounds just from having him in her mouth. On and on she would blow him. Finally his jiz would be streaming out of her mouth... down her neck. But she was greedy... She would take his cock and let him spray his junk all over her titties, and while he laid there spent, she would make him watch her lick his stuff off her tits. Then being totally horny, she would sit on his face, demanding him to eat her pussy. She would straddle his mouth and give him something good to look at – her playing with her tits. He would just get hard all over again. After making her come, over and over again, her screaming his name... She would then lie back and let him fuck her lights out. Over and over again, he would fuck her with his hard cock. Lifting her legs up on his shoulders to enter her more. This would really make her scream until finally he would come all over her belly...*

Well, she might have came in the dream, but in reality, finally, Brad came. He came with his hand hard gripped around his cock. He laid on the couch for a little bit after that. Finally, he got up, got showered, dressed, and headed out the door.

What a great morning!

Chapter Four

Kathy was on her way. She stopped at the Farmer's Market along the way. She picked up some things for lunch. She loved the different artisan's breads and cheeses. She chose a baguette, and some Stilton cheese. There was a liquor store close by, so she stopped in and bottle a bottle of Chablis. She drove her Jaguar to Jean-Luc's house. It was a great house that was about 25 minutes from the city. Jean-Luc loved the Old World look, so that was the décor of the house. Impressionistic paintings, old furniture, totally a classical look. Even his selection of music was either classical or French.

Kathy collected the mail, and put it on the island in the kitchen. The kitchen was great, as that Jean-Luc was a gourmand. Granite counter tops, an indoor grill, all kinds of appliances for the gourmet. She prepared a light lunch of cheese and bread, along with the wine.

She went outside to turn the filter on in the pool, along with the heater. The pool was an underground pool. The backyard was perfectly manicured. Hedges, rose bushes that gave the most incredible fragrance. Of course, there was an herb garden. Jean-Luc loved to cook with fresh herbs. Luckily, while he was away on holiday, the gardener took care of all this. If you further explored the layout of the backyard, there was a gazebo that was set apart, completely furnished with a table and chairs. Jean-Luc at times would invite people over, and entertain outside in the gazebo.

It was a perfect day. Blue skies, warm weather, sunny... Perfect for being outdoors. Plus, Jean-Luc's property was fenced in – total privacy....

Kathy went back in the house, and found a towel, and brought out the wine and her lunch. Finally, not wanting to be a prisoner in her clothes any more, she took off the halter top and the mini skirt, kicking the sandals to the side. She lined the chaise lounge with the towel, donned on her sun glasses and then laid back in the chair.

Occasionally, she drank her wine, just relaxing in the warm sunshine. It was so peaceful... Not a soul in sight...

Chapter Five

While Kathy was relaxing in the sunshine, she was being viewed by a lineman. He couldn't believe as he was fixing an electric line at what he saw. He looked her all over. She was so shapely. Then there were her tits. He liked the way they hung, and how well rounded they were. She had great legs.... The kind that would be great wrapped around a man. Then that shaved pussy....

Justin started to feel a raw power over him. It had been six months since he and Denise broke up. He missed touching a woman. Up until now, he hadn't even really noticed many woman. But this woman was pure fire...

She wasn't even aware that she could be seen. She lay there like a queen. Takes a lot of guts to lay there without a stitch of clothing on... But then she moved.

Kathy had dozed off for a while. Must have been a combination of the sun and the wine. She opened her eyes, and through her sunglasses, she saw a pair of eyes looking at her. She saw him looking her over. His eyes roving all over her body. She liked the admiration in his look. He had nice brown eyes; big strong arms; from the looks of it, very tight abs.. Hmm.... A little company might be nice...

She took the bottle of suntan lotion out of her bag, and laid back in the chaise lounge. She began to smooth it on her chest; down her arms. Up and down motions. She did her legs, her feet. She laid back again, and through the sunglasses, smiled at the man. She began to put more lotion on... she rubbed it between her hands. Then she put the lotion on her chest, and began to work out with each hand going toward a breast. She rubbed the lotion lovingly all over her breast. Slow deliberate strokes, never losing eye contact with the man. She saw him look on with great interest. Finally, after what seemed an eternity, she started rubbing her lotion hands all over her tits.

She began to feel that hot, creamy sensation way down under. She played with her titties endlessly; teasing them and the man. He just looked on like a kid who got what he wanted on Christmas Day. Finally, she let her hands slip slowly down over her abdomen and lower torso. She reached her wet shaved mound. Playfully, she lightly rubbed her hand all over. When she reached for her slit, she ran her finger up and down. Then looking at the man, she deliberately, brought that finger to her lips first licking it, then sucking on the finger like a cock.

She noticed that the man swallowed hard. She liked watching him. Liked that he was watching her. She looked at his cock, and saw that it really needed to come out and play. She took the finger that she sucked on and then motioned to him to come over.

At first he looked amazed. Then he just stood there as if he was deciding what to do. For a minute, she thought he would not accept her invitation. He lowered the bucket truck. For a while she did not see him, until he entered the backyard.

He came over to where she was. He stood over her, taking all of her in. She arose from the chaise, and reached out for him. She brought him towards her, and began to kiss him. She kissed him hard at first, but then, she eased up, little by little. Then, she backed up, and started to undress him. First his shirt. She through it aimlessly in the yard somewhere. Then, she took off his utility belt. She fastened it around her waist. He kind of laughed, but she looked kind of cute, definitely sexy with just his tool belt on. She then ran her hand up and down slowly over his hard on. He put his head back as if to savor her touch. Her teasing tough.... Finally, she slowly unzipped his pants, taking off the pants, and the underwear in one smooth move. He stepped out of them and his shoes. She laid her towel down on the ground. He couldn't believe that they were going to screw right there out in the open. But, she was running the show...

She had him lie down on the towel. The she straddled his face, so he could eat her pussy. She put his hands up to her breasts so that he could give her some titty play. She tasted so good... So damn good. It had been so long. Her tits were nice and hard. He grabbed them, rubbed them... They felt so good. She gyrated all over his face with her wet twat. Her ass shook sexily while as her hips swayed back and forth with his tool belt on swaying, too. She finally came, screaming her release. But he wanted her. Wanted her bad. He wanted to keep making her scream.

When he stopped, she moved to the side, so he could get up. He knelt in front of her and begun to suck her titties. He was like a man on a mission. He grabbed one in each hand, and shoved her tits together. First he licked one, then the other. Then he just licked one and then other in one big circle. When she put her head back moaning, he put both of her tits in his mouth and sucked as hard as he could. She panted hard... Her breaths sporadic. Her pussy was so hot and wet, she couldn't wait for him to fuck her.

When he was done sucking her titties, she went down on his cock. He couldn't believe how she sucked him off with such gusto. He never had it this good with Denise. This woman was a real ball of fire! He was so hard, he was afraid that he would come in her mouth. So he held her head back, and took his cock out of her mouth.

She knelt down on the ground with her perfect ass facing towards him. He entered her wet pussy from behind. Slowly, rhythmically, he fucked her with her wearing his tool belt on from behind. He pumped and pumped his hard, erect cock into her. She panted, he groaned... Finally, he pulled her hair back to have her head towards him. With the other hand he grabbed her left tit. Between fucking her and playing with her titty, she screamed. Over and over again, this went on until he took his cock out of her and came all over her ass. They laid on the towel for a long time with only the warm air to cover them. Each were totally spent.

Then, he got up, put his clothes back on. She leaned up on one arm, still with the sunglasses on and smiled at him. He pointed toward the tool belt. She laughed, and gave it back to him. Each wanted to speak, but the words didn't come. They just looked at one another as if they understood each other. He picked up her available hand, and kissed it. He gave the hand back, and exited the yard.

Denise who?

Chapter Six

Well.... This has turned out to be some day... Who knew?

Kathy laid there by herself for a while. That was what she liked.... Adventure... No commitments... No being tied down. Just getting off and moving on. Damn that felt so good. She liked when he tugged on her hair...

Well, time for this girl to get back to the city before the traffic gets to heavy. She got up, cleaned up her wine glass, quickly showered and dressed.

When Kathy arrived home, she went through the front of the apartment building, and was greeted by the afternoon doorman, Clive. She picked up her mail, and continued on to the elevator. Luckily, as she approached the elevator, it had just come down, and the doors opened. She looked through the mail as she rode up to the fifth floor. A bill, a sexy lingerie catalog, her subscription to Nudearama, and an advertisement for pots and pans.

"Yeah, like I really am going to use those," she laughed aloud, " I'll it save for Jean-Luc. He'll get a kick that I actually got something like this in the mail." Still laughing, she alighted off of the elevator when it came to her floor. She opened the door with her key. As she entered in the doorway to her apartment, she felt her foot trample on something.

"Hello, what do we have here?" Kathy wondered.

It was a cream-colored envelope. Not the cheap kind, but fancy stationery. It wasn't addressed on the front. Kathy went to open the note. It to was on cream-colored stationery. She went on to read:

> Dear Madam,
> *Perhaps you are not aware, but you please need to draw your curtains when entertaining gentleman, or at least wear a robe, as opposed to romping around without clothes on. It is becoming to be a nuisance, and I have to wish to involve the police. Most well brought up people refrain from your way of life.*
>
> Kindly, do be more considerate!
> A Concerned Neighbor

"Fuck you!" swore Kathy.

She then instinctively went to the window. She looked to see who would have the best access to view her apartment. There were two buildings. As she scanned the windows of the apartments, her eye caught a woman looking out the window. She was blonde, short, maybe only about 5"2, with pulled back blonde hair, slim, wearing clothes that were too old for someone her age. The woman looked at her judgmentally with scorn. As if she had seen what she needed to see, she looked at Kathy dismissively, and went away from the window.

"What a bitch!" Kathy said. I'll need to find out who she is, now won't I?

Kathy then purposely took off all of her clothes, laid down on her couch, and grabbed the phone. She called her friend, who she knew could help, Patty.

Chapter Seven

Kathy proceeded to dial up Patty. Patty was a photographer. She did jobs such as model shoots, house/realty shoots, and special occasions.

"Hello," Patty answered the phone.
"Hey girl, what's up?"
"I was just thinking about you."
"Oh you were... That's nice."
"So, what's going on?"
"You know how I don't wear clothes around the apartment?" Kathy asked.
"Yeah."
"Well, this old biddy, who can't be older than 30, got a stick up her ass, and wrote me this note saying I need to wear clothes, and that when I "entertain gentleman," and that I should close my curtains."
"Why doesn't she close her curtains, and why is she watching if she's so disturbed?" asked Patty.
"Exactly," answered Kathy.
"She's probably some dried up old virgin. So, what's the plan?" asked Patty.
"What makes you think there's a plan?" asked Kathy.
"How long have we been friends? I know you too well. There's a plan."
"I need to think about it. How about meeting me for coffee tomorrow, and by then, I should have something in mind? I might need your photography expertise."
"Anything for a friend. When and where?" asked Patty.
"How about Cafe au Lait on fifth and Broadway, say about one?"
"I'll be there."
"Thanks."
"You got it."

"Okay, bitch.... You asked for it!" declared Kathy.

Chapter Eight

Kathy got up, showered and dressed. She wore khaki shorts, and a purple camisole top, with a pair of strappy sandals. The camisole was a nice low cut scoop neck. She went down to the lobby and spoke with the doorman, Alex.

"Good morning, Alex," said Kathy
"Good morning, Ms. Dexter," greeted Alex.
"Alex, I was wondering, do you happen to know anybody who works at the

building across the street?" asked Kathy

"The Windsor, or the Charlemange?"

"The Windsor."

"Yes ma'am, I know Jared, who is the doorman at that building."

"I'm curious about a certain tenant, and I was wondering if he might answer a few questions about the person?"

"What kind of questions?"

"Oh, nothing to detailed. I just wanted to reciprocate a favor that the lady had done for me, but I only know her to see her. I don't know her name." Kathy said.

"Well, that doesn't sound too difficult," said Alex. "I think Jared could help with that."

"Great. You'll never know how much I appreciate your help." said Kathy.

"You're more than welcome Ms. Dexter. That's what I'm here for." offered Alex. "I'll call over to Jared right now. I think he's on duty."

"Wonderful." beamed Kathy.

"Jared, this is Alex over here at the Highlands. I have a tenant who knows one of your tenants, but she only knows the lady to see her, but doesn't know her name. Could she come over, and maybe if she described the lady to you, could you maybe help her?" asked Alex.

"Sure, buddy. Send her over." said Jared.

"Thanks, Jared." said Alex.

"Okay, Ms. Dexter. Jared will help you. He's over there now, and expecting you."

"Thanks again Alex. You're a lifesaver."

"My good pleasure, ma'am."

Kathy crossed the street, and entered the building through the revolving doors. There she saw a young man about 5'8, with curly brown hair and blue eyes, with a name tag that said, "Jared."

"Hello, Jared, I'm Ms. Dexter. Alex from the Highlands just called you about me."

"Yes, ma'am. How may I help you?" offered Jared.

"Well, I'm trying to find out the name of one of your tenants. It's a woman, probably on or about in her late 20's early 30's.... Probably, about 5'2", slender, wears her hair pulled back, blonde hair, kind of...well, she's very "proper." described Kathy.

"Yes, ma'am, I know exactly who you are talking about. Her name is Ms. Cynthia Wentworth." said Jared.

"What can you tell me about her, Jared?" asked Kathy, as she leaned over the podium exposing some of her cleavage.

"Well,"replied a red-faced Jared, "She's very proper as you say. Never any visitors, no children, doesn't go out much, except when she goes to work. She's an administrative assistant for a company. She even has her groceries delivered, as that she doesn't drive."

"So basically, a homebody, no boyfriend, no friends.... no life?" summed up Kathy.

"That's about it, ma'am." qualified Jared.

"What apartment does she live in?"

"I'm sorry ma'am, but that information, I'm not allowed to give out. However, if you just "happened" to go over to the mailboxes, and you just "happened" to see her name on the mailbox with the apartment number on it, that wouldn't be a problem..." Jared winked at Kathy.

"No, it wouldn't," Kathy smiled knowingly at him.

"Just one more question, if you don't mind, Jared?"

"Sure."

"Have you ever noticed anything she ever brought in... maybe a little box of something... Some type of food, or dessert, pastry, something she drinks..." fished Kathy.

"Well, she does like tea, as that I have seen her with a little shopping bag from Tea for Two. Also, She seems to go to Stover's Bake Shop. Never a big box, just a real small one. Something that would fit a dozen small cookies or a cinnamon roll. " volunteered Jared.

"Jared," Kathy said, light touching his arm, "How can I ever thank you? You're the best!" Kathy beamed.

Jared blushed and said, "Oh, I am just glad to help. Come back if you need anything else," he eagerly offered.

"I will." said Kathy as she purposely shook her ass for him to see as she walked to the mailboxes.

Wow, thought Jared.... I'd like to do her in a heartbeat! Look at her...

What an ass... Not to mention those titties of hers. They were just begging to come out of her top and have me make friends with them....Ha, ha....Yeah, I'd like to make friends with every part of her.... Beats looking at these old broads who are bagging and sagging.... Yeah... I'd like to take her for a ride out to beach, and do her on the back of my truck. Nice and slow.... then she could scream my name over and over again... I'd be all over those tits of hers. Look at them... Totally titt-i-licious!

While Jared was day dreaming, Kathy sauntered to the mailboxes. She searched for Cynthia Wentworth's name. Finally, after combing through names, she came to a box marked C. Wentworth, apartment 311.

"Okay, no life, no pets, no boyfriend... Just a work-a-holic, and a bitch. Probably frustrated as hell. No sex life, just works. Probably wears granny pants for underwear," thought Kathy. "This is so on!"

Chapter Nine

Kathy arrived at Cafe au Lait to meet Patty at one o'clock. She saw Patty sitting at a table for two.

"Hey girl." Patty greeted her.

"Hey yourself. Seems like forever since I've seen you."Kathy hugged her. Patty and her had been friends since junior high school. While Patty didn't come from a prestigious family like Kathy, Patty never judged or used her. Patty worked hard for everything she achieved. She put herself through school, and freelances as a photographer. Whenever Kathy needed a favor, Patty was always there in her corner. Patty stood about 5'6, tall, busty, redheaded, green-eyed. She always complained about not being petite. Yet, she always wore clothes that flattered her figure.

After chitchatting about this and that, Patty finally asked her about the note, and the person who sent it.

"Okay, I'm in suspense here. What's with this note you got.?"

"Read it, and you tell me." said Kathy giving her the note.

After reading the note, Patty said,"Okay, I can understand her point a little bit, but at the same time, she should just stick to the facts, and not act like she's better than you. She sounds hypocritical, judgmental, and like she's on some type of soap box. You know what I mean?... Like she needs brought done a peg or two."

"Exactly," said Kathy. "That's why I think she should be taught a lesson, don't you?" "What do you have in mind?" Patty leaned forward with her head resting on her hands.

"Well, I talked with her doorman today. You would have laughed... He's a young kid, who I swear would have jumped down my blouse to feel me up in a heartbeat... At any rate, he told me she's a work-a-holic; no visitors, no kids, no boyfriend, very proper, gets her groceries delivered... Oh, she drinks tea."

"Ooh-la-la," cooed Patty.

"Yeah, I know... Oh yeah... She gets a small box of stuff from a place called Stover's Bake Shop. "

"I know the place. Good stuff. Expensive. But well worth it."

"Well, nothing but the best for Ms. Snitty and Shitty."

Patty swallowed hard, laughing at the same time. "So now what?" "Well," Kathy started, "I'm going to go over to Stover's Bake Shop, and see what Ms. Snitty and Shitty buys.

Then I'm going to buy something for her."

"Are you serious?" Patty asked in amazement, "I wouldn't buy her sh_..."

"Hold on," interjected Kathy. "I'm going to go with pastries in one hand, and let's just say some fruit "punch" in the other hand. Kind of like a peace offering. Hopefully, she'll invite me in. We'll get to talking and drinking. Before you know it, she'll feel very,'relaxed,' in fact, kind of drowsy."

"Why?"
"Because," Kathy explained, "She'll be a little buzzed. In that fruit punch, I'll spike it with something. Remember, she's a tea-totaler. So, she's not used to booze."

"Okay, you get her buzzed, then what?"

"That's where you come in. I'll tell her that your meeting me at her place because we're going out somewhere. When she starts to get buzzed, I'll help her into the bedroom. You're going to come over, with your camera, and let's say we're going to take some interesting pictures of Miss Cynthia. Needless to say, when I put the photos underneath her door, she'll by snitty and shitty no more." Kathy said proudly.

"I love it!" said Patty.

The two friends talked over all the particulars. They agreed that the lady needed this, and that it had to be done. Finally, they parted company about 3:30. Kathy headed back to her apartment.

Chapter Ten

Kathy had just got back in her apartment before it began to rain. She looked quickly through the mail. Bills, catalogs, junk mail.... blah, blah, blah.... She looked at her answering machine, no messages.

She went to the bedroom, and peeled off her clothes. She then looked through her wardrobe to see what she could wear to Ms. Snitty and Shitty's place tomorrow. Hmm... Well... Nothing too revealing.... Okay, maybe some nice slacks, a pink blouse with a little white jacket to go with it. Sounds good. Well, actually a little too demure, but that means Snitty and Shitty will like it. She put the clothes that were on hangers for her to wear tomorrow on a doorknob to hand. Next, to the kitchen for a glass of wine.

She padded naked through the apartment to the kitchen, She poured a glass of white wine. Now, what about the 'punch' for tomorrow? She looked though her liquor selection. What would go with fruit punch? Curcaco would be good... Triple sec as well. And of course, vodka... But not too much "stuff." Don't want to give it away. After all the taste testing I'll have to do, I' might be going there a little buzzed. Kathy laughed lightly.

She walked out to the livingroom with the wine in her hand, and the mail in her other hand. After a while, she happened to look up, and there was a man looking right at her. He was tall, about six foot; ruggedly handsome, dark hair, dark eyes; hmm... must work out... really built. Kathy licked her lips. She then met the man's gaze again. He looked like someone who hadn't eaten in a while. Someone intent in wanting something.

The vixen that she was, Kathy stood up, and walked to the phone. She motioned for the man to call her. She smiled at him. He picked up the receiver. Using her fingers, she gave him the number to dial. Each one laughed while this was going on. Finally, her phone rang.

Chapter Eleven

Brad had been home for a while. He saw Marcey the other night at dinner.
They went to Chez Elle. Dinner was delicious, and he enjoyed hearing her talk about her work. He was still aroused by the woman he had watched across the street. Actually, he couldn't quit thinking about it, or her. At any rate, he was hoping to finally have Marcey stay at his place. They always had to go to her place for intimacy. Brad had been busy since the other day, and finally he was able to come home before ten. He was puttering about when he looked out the window. Again, there was his fantasy woman. He gazed at her for a long while. Just taking all of her in. But then she looked up. There eyes met. There was no escape.... At first he was embarrassed... But admittedly, he couldn't tear his gaze away. She was so confident about herself. Where most women would cover up, she was just so free. Free... she just allowed herself to be; no reservations, no body image problems, she just turned loose. He wished Marcey would be more like that. While he really liked her, and she was sweet, sometimes a guy needs a little fire. This woman was definitely fire.

Uh-oh... She's going to the phone... Is she calling the cops?
Wait a minute... She's motioning for me to pick up the phone. She wants me to call her, I think... Yes, she wants me to call her. She's giving me her phone number. Okay.. 231-602-9563.

"Hi there,"a woman's voice responded.
"Hello," Brad answered.
"My name is Kathy. What's yours?"
"Brad."

"Tell me about yourself, Brad," Kathy said as she went to sit on the couch.

"What would you like to know?"

"What do you do?"

"I sell credit card machines."

"Sounds interesting."

"It has its moments. What about you?" Brad politely asked.

"I don't work if that's what you mean."

"What do you do then?"

"Just living the dream."

Brad smiled, "Just living the dream, huh? Okay....."

"So Brad, did you enjoy watching me the other day?"

"What do you mean?" Brad asked, feeling a little nervous.

"You know... watching me... I liked you watching me..."

"You did?" Brad asked.

"Sure. Not only did I feel good, you watching made it even better."

There was a little bit of silence. Brad didn't know what to say.

"Do you have a girlfriend, Brad, or a Mrs. Brad?" Kathy asked.

"I have a girlfriend."

"What's her name?

"Whose name?"

"Your girlfriend's name."

"Marcey."

"That's nice."

"Thank you. She is very nice."

"That's good. But nice is what you describe an old lady... a librarian... an old grandma. "

"What are you saying?" queried Brad.

"I'm saying, that nice is your mom. Your woman should be a little more than nice."

"Oh... Guess I never looked at it any other way."

"At any rate," said Kathy, "You never answered my other question."

"Which was?"

"Did you enjoy watching me the other day?"

Slowly, he admitted, "Yes."

"So, what now?" She asked.

"What do you mean?"

"Do you want more of what you saw?"

Again, there was silence. Raw, sexual silence.... A million thoughts going through his head... Should he? Should he look away... What to do? What about Marcey?

"Brad?" She asked softly, with parted wet lips.
"Yes, I want more."

"Okay. But.... I want you to come with me." she replied.
"But Marcey..." Brad began to protest.
"No... " she interrupted. "You make you come, while I'm making myself come. Then we both win." She put the phone on speaker phone.

She gazed at him intently. At first he made no move, but then, he too put the phone on speaker phone and took off his shirt. She loved his chest. Bare and very well built. It looked rock hard, and so smooth... She longed to ride her hand up and down it.

Next, he slowly unzipped his pants. He was beginning to get hard. Although she wanted to take care of him in person, she knew she had to be patient. Everything was timing... But she had to start somewhere...

"That's good," she purred. "Very good."

She started to touch her titties. She rubbed them in circles. Enjoying how good her hands felt gliding over them. Around and around... It seemed to go on forever. He looked at her, as if she were a goddess. Amazed at how she just naturally let go... Just was so uninhibited. She felt herself up as if it were the most natural thing to do.

She started her titty play be rolling her tits in between her thumbs and forefingers. Just taking her time, liking the sensations; liking the cream that was starting in her pussy. She wished he were there with her. She tried to imagine his big strong hands handling her titties. Of him licking one and playing with the other... Oh.....

He just kept watching. A familiar ache started in his balls. He started to rub one. Just as she was rubbing her tits, he rubbed his balls... It felt good. No wonder she liked playing with her tits so much. He imagined her sucking on his balls. First one then the other. Then with her greedy lips sucking on both at the same time...

She opened her hooded eyelids to find him totally mesmerized by her. He looked so serious, yet enjoying the show she was providing, and him rubbing his balls. Finally, she needed more stimulation, so she grabbed her tits, and started to squeeze them.

This really turned Brad on. She told him to squeeze his balls the way she was squeezing her tits. He obeyed. The pressure was so good. He got harder and harder. He wanted her so badly.

She looked at him boldly. She picked first one titty up and brought it up to her mouth to lick it. First, she just flicked the tit with her tongue. Then, she began to suck it as hard as she could. She was trying to imagine him there licking, sucking and biting at her titties. She rubbed her legs together instinctively, and began to feel her juices oozing.

She then started with the next titty. Doing the same thing. Never losing eye contact with him. It felt so damn good... Finally, the ecstasy over took her, making her close her eyes, and tilt her head back.

She was amazing he thought. If only Marcey would act like this sometimes... Marcey... don't want to think about her right now... This feels too good.
"My titties are so hard, and my pussy is so wet for you, Brad."
"Baby, you're amazing," Brad breathed hard.

She finally gave him what he wanted. She started to play with her shaved twat. First, she just traced her oozing slit. Her finger slid so easily up her creamy seam. Her juices were so hot and sticky. What she would give for his tongue to be there instead of her finger..... mmm... It feels so good. "I wish you were here to eat my pussy..."

She looked over at him. He started to feel up his cock. It was rock hard by now. He was trying to keep looking at her, but was getting caught up in his own arousal.

She was trying to pace herself, but Kathy was starting to feel an urgent need to come. It was overpowering her to keep a steady rhythm. What with her hard titties, wet pussy, and him groping his cock and balls.... It was too much... she needed to come... Now and badly!

She took her free hand, and started to play with her titty, while with the other hand finger fucking her hot, wet, cunt. Her finger found her engorged clit, The feeling was intense.... almost more than what could she could bear.... It was pleasure and pain all at the same time. She wanted more! She rubbed her clit as hard as she could, screaming, "Oh my titties, oh my pussy!."

He watched her... He loved how she talked dirty... How she made herself come. How she was making him hard without even touching him. Just the power of her...

As she came each time more intensely than the next, he pumped his cock harder and harder. Her screaming her orgasm, and masturbation , plus his own manipulation made him start to come. He could feel the tightness of his cock. It was if he could not carry his burden any more. Just too big... Needed release.. Needed it now.

Finally, he jerked on his cock harder and harder until he gasped his orgasm, and his jiz oozed out of the head of his cock.

Each lay totally spent. The release had come; the dam had been broken, and the floodgates let out... Each going through their own storm, and now... experiencing the calm...

Finally, it was Kathy who spoke."That was great!"
"It sure was," Brad said softly.
"No regrets?"
"No... None." replied Brad.
"See you around sometime?" Kathy questioned.
"Sure." Brad responded.
"Good night, Brad."
"Good night, Kathy."

Kathy went over to hang up the phone, and then to turn off the wall light. She then headed for the bedroom.

Brad himself got up off the couch, hung up the phone, and turned off his lights as well. He then headed for the shower. It was a long shower. He was washing himself, yet let the water run over him for a while. He felt so liberated; so free. Almost as if he climbed a mountain. Seriously... How many men get to have an experience like this? He didn't know how to feel. In one respect, he felt bad about Marcey; yet, it was so good, it was hard to feel bad. And it wasn't as if he actually screwed the woman. So, what harm was actually done?

He climbed in bed and went blissfully asleep.

Chapter Twelve

Kathy got up showered and dressed. She put on the outfit that she chose from last night. Last night... Boy that Brad was sure something... Patience... Patience...
At any rate, She had a lot of things to do... Let's see. Have to go to Stover's Bake Shop, grocery store, and the liquor store. She grabbed her purse and headed to the bakery shop.

Kathy drove to the bakery. She parked her car right in front of the shop. It was a cute little place, with big widows and planter boxed of colorful flowers. She went into the shop, and peered at the endless line of display cases.

"Hello and welcome to Stover Bake Shop. May I help you with something?" inquired a nice salesgirl. "Yes," replied Kathy. "There's a lady who comes here, and I'm meeting with her today, but I don't know what she gets." "What's her name? Maybe she places an order." offered the salesgirl. "Her name is Cynthia Wentworth."

The salesgirl's face went from a smile to a frown.

"Yes, the lady buys from here."
"What does she typically buy?" asked Kathy.
"Petit fours."
"Great, I'd like a dozen of them," requested Kathy. "And also, in separate boxes please, one dozen cookies assorted. Thank you."

The salesgirl boxed everything, and rang up the purchase, which Kathy paid for. Curious to know what the salesgirl knew, Kathy said, "I hope Miss Wentworth will like these petit fours. She can be so difficult to please sometimes."

The salesgirl smiled a knowing smile at Kathy.

Kathy continued, "I guess I kind of got on the bad side of the lady, and so I'm trying to make it up to her. She's a touch cookie, isn't she?" "You can say that again," agreed the salesgirl, named Sarah. "She's hard to please," fished Kathy. "I don't mind trying to please someone," said Sarah, "but she's very standoffish, and no matter what you do, or how you do it, she never is pleased, or says thanks."

"Okay, now she's a pain in the ass to people," thought Kathy

"Well, thank you very much, Sarah."
"Please come again, ma'am."

Just as Kathy was gathering up her purchases, a baker came from the back. He was tall, broad shouldered, very muscular, with hazel eyes. They caught each others eye, and held each others gaze. Finally he put down the tray of bread he was carrying. She heard him say to Sarah, "Sarah, slice these pullman loaves for Sylvie's Restaurant. Someone will be here soon to pick them up." "Okay, Joe," said Sarah. Joe gave Kathy a look, and then went back to the production area to work. She definitely would be back to Stover Bake Shop.

Kathy then went to the liquor store to pick up the rum, and the grocery store to pick up the items for the punch. When she returned to her apartment, she saw Alex, and said, "Hi, Alex." "Hello, Ms. Dexter." "Here, I wanted to bring you something for all your help the other day." "Thank you very much, Ms. Dexter. That was very thoughtful of you." Kathy smiled at him and walked into the opening elevator door. She went up to her apartment, and started mixing the punch together. "Let's see... pineapple juice, cranberry raspberry juice, sweetened lime juice, lemon-lime soda, and the piece de resistance, rum. She poured it into a decorative container, filled with ice. Kathy got her things together, and headed out again.

She walked into the Windsor, and saw Jared, the doorman.

> "Why hello, Ms. Dexter."
> "Hello, Jared. These are for you. I really appreciated your help the other day."
> "You didn't have to do that, but thank you very kindly."
> "You're most welcome."

Kathy walked away. But then she couldn't resist. So she put a little saunter into her step, and a wiggle in her ass... Jared definitely noticed. She couldn't help but smile to herself, while he thought, *"Yeah, I'd like to have a piece of that ass."*

Kathy got onto the elevator, now only with her purse, the punch and the box of petit fours. She got off of the third floor, and headed to Miss Cythia's door. She knocked at the door. At first she didn't hear anything, but then she heard slight movement." There was definitely someone coming.

The door opened. There she was... face to face with Cynthia Wentworth.

She was very old looking for her really young age. Her hair tied back so severely, it looked as if it hurt. She coldly looked at Kathy, and said, "Yes."

> "Hello Ms. Wentworth. My name is Kathy Dexter."
> "Yes, I know who you are. What do you want?" Cynthia nastily asked.
> "I guess the opportunity to talk with you, and smooth things over."
> *"What a bitch!" though Kathy.*
> "There's no need for that."
> *"Oh please, I really would like to talk with you."*

Kathy held up the box with the Stover Bake Shop logo on it, along with the punch.

> *"Peace offering," said Kathy.*
> *"What's in the box?"*
> *"Petit fours, and I have some delightful fruit punch."*
> *"Well, perhaps she's not totally hopeless, and might have some class yet,"* thought Cynthia.
> "Very well, do come in."

Chapter Thirteen

The apartment was white all over, and totally immaculate. Everything perfectly in place.

"Do sit down." said Cynthia

"Thank you."

"It would appear that I've offended you some how," offered Kathy, "And, since we're neighbors, I figured we could talk things over, and begin anew."

"Well, I really don't know what there is to say," Cynthia stuffily said.

"Perhaps, if we got to know one another, that would be a start." suggested Kathy.

"Perhaps," sniffed Cynthia.

"Okay, then, tell me about yourself, Ms. Wentworth."

"I am an Administrative Assistant for Mr. Gerald Tolliver, at Keystone International. I'm sure you have heard of the organization."

"Yes," replied Kathy. "I have. Do go on."

"Well, I see to Mr. Tolliver's correspondences, meetings, schedule, arrange affairs, deal with vendors, staff and a potpourri of other tasks as well."

"Sounds like you have a lot on your plate, and that you practically run the place," Kathy complimented her.

"Yes, I do a good job."

"Do you like what you do?"

"I'm good at what I do."

"But do you like it? Do you like your job."

"I don't consider it a job. I consider it my position in the company." Cynthia said devoid of any feelings.

"My God... This woman is like a robot. Maybe it's her upbringing. But how could two parents screw up a kid this badly?" pondered Kathy.

"I see," replied Kathy. Looking around the room, Kathy said, "You have a lovely apartment. Did you decorate it yourself?"

"I chose the décor, and had a decorator do the work."

"I like the painting. Who is the artist?"

"Manet. It's an impressionistic work of art."

"Well, ooh-la-lah,"thought Kathy.

"It's lovely and really compliments your apartment."

"Thank you." said Cynthia.

"Oh, I did bring these little dainties from a shop called Stover Bake Shop. Perhaps you've heard of it," smiled Kathy. "Yes, I have," perked up Cynthia. Cynthia eyed the box like a dog waiting for a treat. "I wasn't sure what you liked, so I figured I couldn't go wrong with some petit fours." lied Kathy. Well, Kathy couldn't believe that's what it took to get some warmth out of this frigid personality. "Yes, they are just fine," Cynthia almost showing a smile. Too bad... She actually looked nice when she smiled even if just a glimpse of a smile. "Oh, and I brought some fruit punch for us to have with our tea dainties," beamed Kathy. "It's a family recipe that I couldn't wait to share with you." *"Yeah, bitch, it's punch alright; it's going to punch out your tea-totalling snitty shitty ass on the ground!"*

The ladies had their punch and tea dainties, and formally conversed about general topics. Luckily, Cynthia was enjoying the punch as well, and enjoyed several cups of the fruit concoction. She said, "This really is delicious. What's in it?" "Well," said Kathy, "It is a family secret, but, I can tell you it has cranberry-raspberry juice, sweetened lime juice, and lemon-lime soda, and pineapple juice." Okay, so I didn't mention the part about the rum. Ha, ha, ha..... She'll figure that out tomorrow.... The thought of this bitch hung over was hilarious!

After awhile, Kathy could tell that Cynthia was getting buzzed. The woman actually became human, and was laughing and giggling. If only she could keep this lady like this. All the same, the plan was working. Finally, Cynthia's eyes were growing heavy. She said to Kathy, "I feel so sleepy." "Are you well, Ms. Wentworth?" feigned Kathy. "Yes, quite, just sleepy." "Well," offered Kathy, "Perhaps, I could help you into your bedroom, then I'll clean up our tea dishes, and I will let myself out." "Yes, that sounds good." agreed Cynthia.

Chapter Fourteen

Kathy came over to where Cynthia was sitting, and helped her to stand up. Cynthia was very wobbly on her feet, so Kathy had her put her arm around Kathy's shoulder to help balance her. Luckily, Cynthia was very lithe, and easy to help. She walked towards the back of the unit, until they reached the bedroom.

The bedroom, like the rest of the living space, was just as immaculate. This room, too, was done up in white and champagne colors with golden accessories. Very prominent and classical. She laid Cynthia down on the bed, with her head to lay on the decorative satin pillow. Then, she brought Cynthia's legs up onto the mattress. "Thank you for helping me, and coming over. Sorry to take ill like this." said a very nice Cynthia. "Oh, no problems. Hope you're feeling better, and that we can do this again." offered Kathy. With that, Cynthia was out for the count. She fell fast asleep.

Kathy went back to the living room, and hurriedly, but quietly cleaned up the tea dishes. She then went to check on Cynthia. She was dead to the world. She text Patty to come over. Patty was on the way. She then began to undress Cynthia. She undid the little pearl buttons on her blouse, finally opening the garment to expose her in a bra. The bra was white and ordinary. No lace, no bows... Just as utilitarian as its owner. She couldn't be any more than an A cup. She was able to lift Cynthia towards her without waking her, watching for a text from Patty to know if she arrived at the door yet. She then after removing the woman's bra, and blouse, laid her back on the pillows. She then undid the skirt, slip and granny panties that the woman was wearing. Stockings were next. Cynthia never budged. She lay there naked as the day she was born.

Kathy looked at her. She gently removed the pins that held Cynthia's hair a pristine hostage, Her blonde hair splashed out onto the pillow. Actually, looking at her, she was quite lovely to behold. Her skin was white and clear; and her nipples the color of delicate pink rosebuds. Her mound was unshaven.

Kathy's phone vibrated. Patty text her that she was at the door.

Kathy went to answer the door. She quietly let her in. They crept back to the bedroom. Patty efficiently set up her camera and what was needed. Kathy stripped out of her clothes and lay down next to Cynthia. Patty then helped with positioning them both to get the most realistic shots possible.

Patty positioned Kathy to be kissing Cynthia's neck. From there, she had Kathy put her lips on Cynthia's. She was even able to get a shot of Kathy's tongue in Cynthia's mouth. Cynthia stirred, and Kathy smoothed her hair as if comforting a child. Kathy motioned to Patty that everything was okay, and to continue. She started to kiss Cynthia's chest. Then she started to play with her rosebud nipples. She first rubbed it with her hand, then she licked it. She liked the thoughts of what she was doing to Cynthia. She wondered what it would be for this frigid woman to actually climax. To make her moan, want, pant.....

Kathy then put her mouth over the now hardening nipple and began to suck on it. Patty was getting some really great shots. She repeated this to the other nipple. Finally, she began to give Cynthia butterfly kisses over her belly. She must have liked this, because Cynthia began to sigh, and turned her head with a smile on it. She kissed her way down to Cynthia's warm soft mound. Kathy opened up her moist labia, and showed it to the camera. Then, she posed having her finger in Cynthia's wet slit. Kathy then, bent toward the mound, and put her tongue in Cynthia's sweet spot. For some reason, Kathy really had to hold back. She wanted to make this woman come.... make her scream.. have control over her. She started to lick her. Cynthia's hands moved instinctively towards Kathy's head. While Kathy wanted to eat her out, fortunately, Patty, sensing something was up, touched Kathy's shoulder.

The photos went on and on... One with their mounds touching. One with their titties touching. Then Patty gently took the pillow away from Cynthia's head. She positioned Kathy to almost be sitting on Cynthia's face. With that, she had Cynthia's head turned from the camera, and Kathy held Cynthia's hand up to her titty. Patty then had Kathy in a 69 position with Cynthia. The final pose was the two of them cuddling, with Kathy's leg draped over Cynthia's. They hurriedly, but quickly put Cynthia under the covers, got Kathy re-dressed, and scattered Cynthia's clothing over the bedroom floor.

They made sure everything was in tact and the way it should be. They locked the door, and left.

Chapter Fifteen

Kathy went back over to her apartment, and Patty went back to her studio to develop the film. She couldn't wait for Patty to come back with the pictures. She was literally on pins and needles. Oh well, may as well get the note and envelope ready . Hmm.... What to say.....

> *Dear Cynthia,*
> *Just a remembrance of our afternoon together. Hope we can do it again* soon. *Hope you enjoyed it as much as I did.*

> Kathy

There.. Done... Where is Patty?

Just then, the apartment intercom buzzed. "Hello?" inquired Kathy.
"Let me in," said Patty. Kathy buzzed her in. Within minutes Patty was in the apartment.

> "How did they turn out?"
> "You tell me," Patty handed her the envelope with the pictures.

Kathy took the envelope and opened it. They were good. Convincing. It actually looked like they had slept together.

> "This is great."
> "When are you going to send them to her?" asked Patty.
> "In a couple of days. I want her still to feel in control of the situation."
> "What are you going to do?"
> "Here read this."

After Patty read the note, she said, "Smooth... Very smooth.. I like it because it forces her to look at the pictures to see what you mean." "Exactly," said Kathy

"Let's have some wine and celebrate," said Kathy.
"Let's." agreed Patty.

They talked forever about how they couldn't get over that the pulled the whole thing off. It was amazing that Cynthia never woke up.

"For a minute, I thought you really liked her," said Patty
"I almost, and that's the opportune word, felt sorry for her. But she's just so damn snotty. Otherwise, it seems like she's her own prisoner"
"Do you want to do her?" asked Patty.
"Why?"
"Just curious."
"Yeah... why not... I wouldn't mind making her scream the roof off."
"Well, actually," started Patty reaching out for Kathy, "I wouldn't mind screaming myself." She brought Kathy to her, and kissed her.

Chapter Sixteen

Kathy and Patty had been on and off. Kind of friends with benefits. No boundaries, no commitments, just simple. It suited both of them, but they could always talk about anything.

Patty kissed Kathy. She was so horny from watching Kathy with Cynthia. Her thong panties have been wet since. She just wants to get off. Kathy responded back. She too was horny after touching Cynthia, and no action. Her titties have been tingling, and her twat throbbing with need for release. Slowly Patty stood up, and piece by piece she stripped in the living room for Kathy. Then she kissed Kathy again.

Their kisses were deep, with their tongues swirling in each others' mouths. Patty started to try and free Kathy from her blouse. She pulled the front zipper down, and out popped Kathy's titties. Kathy shrugged out of the nuisance garment. She wanted to be free of her clothes. The blouse was thrown somewhere in the livingroom. Patty began to nuzzle Kathy's neck. Kathy breathed in a sigh. Patty worked her way down. She started to play with Kathy's titty. Kathy drew in a breath. She then whispered in Kathy's ear," I've been thinking about this all day." She then sucked one tit, and kept playing with the other. Kathy's pussy was creamy all over again. Then, Patty pushed Kathy's tits together, and began to suck both at the same time. Kathy thought she would explode. She reached to stroke Patty's titty through her shirt. "Tell me," said Kathy coming up for air, "What do you want to do to me?" Her lips returned to Kathy's tits.

"I wan to eat that pussy of yours. I want to stick my fingers inside of you, and rub you until you come. I want to lick my fingers.

"Mmm..." Patty purred, "I want that too. But right now, I want your pants off."

Between her and Patty, Kathy's pants were tossed aside. Kathy never wore underwear, so Patty had easy access to Kathy's pussy. Leaving Kathy's titties, she kissed her way down to Kathy's shaved mound. She got off the couch and slid down in front of her wet pussy.

"Play with your tits. Give me something good to look at."
Kathy did as she was told. Then she began to feel Patty's warm, moist tongue, teasing her hot slit. She moaned with passion. It felt so good, so damn good. Kathy started to claw at the couch. Patty had to grab onto Kathy's hips to steady her. Finally, Patty could hold back no longer. She buried her face in Kathy's hot, wet twat, and licked her for all she was worth. She was merciless in her assult of Kathy's clit with her tongue. She came over and over, for what seemed like forever. Kathy never though her clit would stop throbbing. Then Patty stopped eating her, and fingerfucked her endlessly. On and on her finger thrusted in and out of Kathy's drenched hole. Patty would say to her, "Cock or pussy?" You like cock, but you love pussy." Patty repeated this over and over again, until Kathy screamed with orgasm, "Pussy! Pussy!"

She let her have a temporary break. She got up, and went to her big over the shoulder bag. She pulled out a big black two way strap on dildo. She inserted the one end into her wet cunt. She then went over to Kathy.

"Suck it." she commanded Kathy.

Kathy licked her lips, and did as she was told. She got up on her knees while Patty took her place on the couch. She blew Patty as if she were blowing a guy. While she was doing this, Patty began licking her titties never losing eye contact with Kathy. The electricity between them crackled in the air. Finally, Patty put her hand on Kathy's head, and gently pulled in off the dildo. "Look at you.. Look at your spit all over my dick,"she said in a husky voice, "Fuck your tits on my cock."

Kathy took her hard titties and pushed them around the Patty's cock. She could feel how wet her pussy was. The juices were all over her thighs. She rubbed her tits up and down that hard cock. Over and over again. Up and down she slid her tits. Patty reached out and squeezed Kathy's hard tits with her hands, making Kathy cry out loudly.

Kathy felt like her cunt was on fire. It longed to be satisfied, and she didn't care how. She liked Patty's power over her.

"Get on top, and fuck my cock." Kathy who was so wet and horny, got on, and inserted the cock into her wet, creamy, hot cunt. She straddled Patty who laid on the floor, getting fucked, and played with her own tits.

Kathy rocked back and forth, bringing them both into a frenzy. Each one screamed for their own orgasm. Kathy's tits bouncing up and down, and Patty's titties going up and down, too.

"Fuck... Fuck yeah!"
"Yeah baby, yeah... Fuck me hard... harder... Yeah, Oh... Oh... Oh!!"

Finally when they were spent, Kathy fell over, laying on top of Patty. When Kathy could get up, she got off the dildo, and then began to unstrap in off of Patty. She threw it to the side. She lay back down over Patty on her belly, facing Patty's pussy. She threw her hair back, and began to tongue Patty's slit. Patty felt her pussy lips being tonged, and started to put her face into Kathy's hot twat. She wasn't through making her scream yet.

Kathy licked and licked Patty. At times, she would work Patty's pussy with her fingers. Sometimes, she would even spank Patty's pussy. Patty would just get creamier and creamier.

Patty, would finger play Kathy's twat with one hand, and lick the crack of her ass. Then she would spank Kathy's ass cheek hard with her free hand.

Each woman came over and over again. It was as if they couldn't get enough of each other. Again, spent, they finally laid on the floor cuddling each other.

"Shit.." Kathy said.
"That was so fucking good," Patty said as she kissed Kathy on the mouth.

Finally they got up, and Patty got dressed. Standing their nude, Kathy said, "Aren't you staying over?" "No," said Patty, "Remember, no commitments. It's better that I don't stay." She packed up her dildo, and hugged and kissed Kathy. But before she left, she put her finger inside Kathy's wet cunt. She pulled it out and brought it to her lips saying, "One for the road." "Yeah, but I want it back," said Kathy, as she grabbed Patty, and put her tongue in her mouth. Patty grabbed Kathy's ass, and squeezed it as hard as she could. Then she left.

Chapter Seventeen

Kathy awoke the next morning. She was always happy to start the day. The day always led to many an adventure. That's what made life fun. Always adventure; always surprises; always something to be had. Then there were people like Cynthia, whose life she wouldn't want for anything. Seemed like the woman was trapped in her own hell. Then there was Brad; a nice enough guy, yet stuck in a relationship that clearly he was going through the motions with. Where was the spark? The passion? Seemed like you could get more from the vegetables at the Produce Department.

Kathy was still thinking about the guy at Stover Bake Shop. Joe. What a you know Joe? Kathy giggled to herself. She was going to go there today. She wouldn't mind being his little cream puff. He he he... She liked him; something mysterious and masterful about him. She got up, and went out into the livingroom toward the kitchen. She wanted a glass of orange juice. She got the juice, and brought it into the living room. She sat down with pen and paper writing a list of what had to be done this week.

1. Joe   (Ha, ha, ha....)
2. Cynthia (Ha, ha, ha, ha)
3. Brad (Hopefully)

Brad... She hadn't seen him in a while... She looked over at his window. Oh my God! There he was. She waved to him, totally nude. She motioned for him to pick up the phone and call her. She started to put her fingers up to give him the phone number, but he raised a hand in the air, as if to say, "I have the number."

Ring went the phone.
"Well, good morning sunshine," cooed Kathy.
"You're awful chipper," said Brad.
"I love mornings. Everyday is an adventure to be had."
"That's an interesting point of view." said Brad.
"So, what's up? How's it going?" asked Kathy
"Okay. How about you?"
"Not bad. How's your girfriend, Mary?"
"Marcey."
"Sorry. I knew it was something like that."
"She's okay. Actually she's coming over tonight."
"What's the big plans."
"We'll go out to dinner then come back. Typical evening." but Brad had a big smile on his face.
"For typical, you sure seem happy about it. Come on.. Give. What's up?"
"Well, typically, we have to stay at her place. I finally got her to agree to

stay here tonight." said Brad.

"Sounds interesting. But what if we made it really interesting?"

"What do you mean we, and what's on your mind?"

"Look, your hang up with doing me, is that you don't want to cheat on her. But, what if you could have both of us, so to speak, at the same time?"

"She wouldn't be into a threesome."

"I'm not talking that... Well... Not exactly."

"What do you mean then," Brad asked with curiousity.

"Well, let's say you're with her, but yet, you could see me, just like what we did the other night. You take care of her needs, and you watch me take care of mine. That could really be hot... If you wanted to, you could do to her, what I'm doing to me. She would never be the wiser. It would be like doing the both of us at the same time, but without the drama or the guilt." Kathy eagerly explained.

"I don't know......What if she caught on?" asked Brad.

"Look, Brad, if she's having an orgasm, she's only concerned about her at that time. Nothing else will matter. Come on... What do you say?"

Brad thought about it... *"You lucky bastard! Jackpot... Do you know how many guys would want to be in your shoes right now?"* "Okay, but she's not going to let me do her in my living room." "No problem," said Kathy. "I can see your bedroom from here. Just keep her on an angle, so I can see her, but she can't see me. What time?" "We should be back about nine." said Brad. "Make sure she drinks a little wine. That way she'll be nice and relaxed." offered Kathy. "Okay," said Brad, "I have to go to work now, but I'll see you later." "Bye. Have a nice day," said Kathy brightly.

"Yeah baby. I'll see you and your little Cinderella later. Just a little bit more time and patience... You'll want to do me yet." Kathy gloated to herself. *"I'll be dining on Tube Steak at Brad's Place... and enjoying a Brad protein shake coming out of my mouth... he he he... What a bad girl you are Kathy!... But I love it all the same!"*giggled Kathy.

"Now, time for me to hopefully do the baker man."

Chapter Eighteen

Kathy finally got dressed and headed out the door. The day was going to be an exciting day. She had a few errands to do today. She wanted to pick up some more wine, some bath salts, a new toy, maybe even a hot teddy or leather bustier.. Some eye candy for Brad; then she would strip as he was doing Cinderella Mary or Marcey, or whatever the hell her name was.... No, she wasn't jealous of the girl. She just wanted the challenge of doing Brad. The thought of him fucking her with that cock of his.... Mmmm.... she was starting to get moist all ready. *"Down girl!"* she reminded herself, *"First the baker, then the neighbor."*

She was walking towards the shop. She was wearing a low cut sleeveless blouse, with a short mini skirt and pumps. She never wore underwear. She entered the shop.

She looked around until a salesgirl came over to her. "Oh, hello. How did you like what you bought the other day?" "Everything was absolutely delicious," said Kathy. In fact, I have an order, but I would like to speak with the baker if I may. I believe his name is Joe." "Yeah, Joe," said the salesgirl, "Ill call him on the intercom."

"Joe?" paged the girl, "I have a customer here who wants to talk to you about an order." "Tell the customer I'll be right there," answered Joe.

Within minutes, Joe appeared. She remembered him well from the other day. She saw in his expression that he remembered her from the other day. "Joe," said the salesgirl, "This is the lady who wanted to speak with you." "Thank you. I'll take care of her from here."Joe said as he looked at Kathy with a grin.

"Yes ma'am. What can I do for you?" asked Joe.
"Give me some of that cock, baker man." thought Kathy.
"I have a big order, which I believe only you, I mean, your shop can fill."
"Come on in the back, so that we can talk without being interrupted. Sarah, please hold all calls, and tell the vendors I'll call them later with the orders."

"You got it, Joe." said Sarah.

He led her to the back production room. Lots to see... work tables, mixers, a huge oven, and equipment that *she had no clue what the use would be.*

"I knew you would be back." said Joe.
"You seem sure of yourself."
"Am I wrong?"
"No."
"So, 'ma'am," he drawled. "What's your big order that only my shop can fill?" he asked amused.
"Well," she slowly advanced towards him, "It is a **big** order. Do you think you can fill it?" she asked teasingly.
" I can fill it and then some," claimed Joe, smiling like a wolf.

She came towards him, and he drew her towards him. He kissed her deeply, as she ran her hands up and down his white baker shirt. Finally, she started to undo the buttons on his shirt, as he felt her up.

She had been thinking about this for days... Her pussy was oozing with desire. He played with her titties through her blouse. Oh he was good... He knew how to give good titty play... Finally, tired of of her blouse, he undid the zipper, and cast the garment aside. He then undid her skirt, as it swished lightly to the ground. She stepped out of the skirt. He grabbed her by the waist and put her on the bench. He went back to her, kissing her, and rubbing her titties. He rolled and rolled her tits. It was so good. Wonder if he rolled the dough this way?

Finally, he laid her down on the bench, where he began to suck her tits. First he sucked one, and played with the other. Then he changed hands. He then stopped, walked away, and came back with two covered bowls. One was filled with custard; the other looked like a raspberry filling of some type. He smeared one tit with the custard, and the other one with the raspberry. She felt so decadent; so totally naughty. He licked her titties clean. She threw her head back enjoying the feeling of being totally savoured. *"Oh yeah... lick me... fuck me.... I need to come so badly!"The tension was growing!*

Finally, he kissed his way down past her stomach... He stopped. Put the bowls to the side. He then went over to the cooler. He pulled out another bowl. He came back and put the bowl next to her. He looked deep into her eyes. Then he went back to kissing her down the length of her body. Just then he found her hot, oozing slit. He flicked it back and forth with his tongue. It seemed like he would keep her in suspense forever. She tried to bring her hand down and rub her clit, but he slapped her hand away. She thought she would die if she didn't come soon! He licked and licked... She tried again to get at her clit, but again, he slapped the offending hand away... *"Whack!"Earning* her a hard slap on the ass. Finally, he held her hand down with his own. Baker Joe was in charge!

She rolled back and forth over the bench. She looked up threw lidded eyes to see him looking at her with a look of dominance and satisfaction with himself. Oh yeah, he was the man.... The Baker Man, baby.... and don't forget it!

He then started to finger fuck that wet, hot pussy of hers. She started to come. She moaned and panted. On and on, he brought out more screams from her, than she could remember. She tried to count every time she had an orgasm, but couldn't keep track. Finally, he relented... Temporarily....

He put his hand in the covered bowl he got out of the cooler. He slapped it all over her wet, creamy cunt, making it even creamier. It was something light, yet cool... He opened her wet pussy lips to get the concoction inside of her. Her engorged clit ached at the cold feeling.... He then opened her up, and buried his face in her creamy, steamy twat.

This brought about new screams and sensations. Oh he was good... He was so damn good! He new how to get a woman off! This guy should write books, and do movies.... Oh my God!

When he was done playing with her, he helped her up off the bench. He picked her up off the bench, brought her roughly to him, and began to suck her titties again. He had to hold her to support her, as that she was trembling from head to toe. Her body was reeling from all the orgasms and sensations. Not satisfied with all he had done, he made her stand up, while he shoved his fingers back in her wet, aching twat... *She thought she would die.... The sensations... her titties, her pussy.... her clit.... Her aching clit!*

He whispered in her ear," What a bad girl you are.... But you like being a bad girl don't you? You like custard and raspberry filling on your titties, and whipped cream in that hot pussy of yours, don't you?" ... She didn't answer him at first. "He then whispered in her ear again, more intently, "Don't you/?" "Yes, I'm a bad girl, and I like it. I like it a lot!" He whispered in her ear, "Let's see how bad a girl you really are."

He had her stand facing the bench, with her hands on the bench. With his foot, he had her spread her legs wide. She could feel the juices coming down her thighs. This was so hot!

"Bad girl deserves a spanking. Actually, a lot of spankings. Count each one." Joe commanded.
> Whack! "One."
> Whack! "Two."
> Whack! "Three."
> Whack! "Four."
> Whack! "Five,"

He then started with the other ass cheek.
> "Count," he ordered.
> Whack! "Six."
> Whack! "Seven."
> Whack! "Eight."
> *Whack! "Nine."*
> *Whack! "Ten."*

Her cunt was dripping wet at this time. He commented as he rubbed her slick slit from behind.

"Look at you.. Your pussy is dripping wet! What do you have to say for yourself?" he hissed in her ear.

"I'm a little slut who needs discipline."
"Who else have you fucked?'"
"My neighbor lady, my friend, a utility worker, tonight I'll be doing myself, while watching my neighbor do his girlfriend."
"You are a little slut! Have you done the neighbor with the girlfriend?"
"No, but I want to."
"Little, dirty slut.... You definitely need more discipline."

She heard him unzipper his pants. The sound filled the room as she stood there eagle spread. Then she heard, and felt the crack of his folded belt against her ass...

Crack! "Count, he ordered."
"One."
Crack. "Two."
Crack. "Three."
Crack. "Four."
Crack. "Five."
Then he changed sides.
Crack. "Six." *"Oh God... It feels so good. Oh I need him to fuck me*
bad!" Crack. "Seven."
Crack. "Eight."
Crack. "Nine."
Crack. "Ten."

She screamed out. "Oh!!!."
"What's a matter ?... You're pussy aching for me to fill you up with this?"
He put his hard, bare, cock against her ass.
She didn't answer. He jerked her, and she said. "Yeah, I want that hard cock in my wet, pussy. I want it now!.."

"You'll" get it. But when I'm ready to give it for you."
He then rubbed his hand over her red ass cheeks. He spread her ass cheeks and put whipped cream on his hands. He spread the cream all over the crack of her ass. He then licked her ass. Between the whipped cream and the feel of his tongue, she thought she would come all over again.

He then turned her around. She looked down at his hard cock.

"Suck it." he said.

She got down on her knees in front of him. She sucked his cock there in the bake shop. She held her head down. Back and forth, back and forth she sucked. When he was near to climaxing, he had her stop, by pulling her head back. He helped her stand up. She stood her again facing the bench. He took his hard cock and fucked her dripping cunt from behind. He pounded that pussy as hard as he could. He heard her scream over and over again. Finally, he took his cock out of her, and shot the cum all over her face and tits. She welcomed his jiz with joy. She couldn't get enough... Even tried to suck his cock again.

He was totally spent. She stood there with his junk all over her. He told her to rub it into her tits, and he wanted to watch her lick it off. She did as he told her. He reached over, and gave her a towel, and had her clean herself up at the hand sink.

He shucked on his pants, and sat on a stool, as she dressed. He led her out to the display area, where he originally found her.

"Well, ma'am, thank you for the order. I hope I was able to satisfy you."
"Oh you did. You really did." Kathy smiled wickedly.

Joe went back to the production area. He turned off all the cameras that were rolling. He knew she would come.

Chapter Nineteen

Wow! What a day, and it's not over yet. Kathy kept thinking about Joe. How he handled her. How he had total control over her. It was so sexy. He really understood her. She wouldn't mind having another go round from him! He fucked her with such force. The spanking and whipping was totally unexpected, but totally loved! "I'm still wet,"Kathy thought. She had errands to do, and had to do them with a wet pussy, and hard titties. Her thighs slick with her juices, and the smell of sex. She thought of Joe's hard cock in her mouth. She could suck him forever! Mmm......

She picked up some votive candles; vanilla, and sandalwood. Then the bath crystals. She saw a flower vendor and picked up some red roses. Then to buy some lingerie and toys... She bought a leather bustier, a jelly dong, and she couldn't help it, a leather flogger. She really liked the feel of being whipped with Joe's belt. The wine was the last thing on the list. She got a red wine. She like the name of the wine. It had strawberry, kiwi in the red wine.

She got home with all her packages. She put the wine in the fridge. The flowers in a vase, except for three roses. She then drew a bath with the bath salts, and laid out the lingerie and the small flogger on the bed. While the water was running, she lit candles around the living room, and the bathroom. When the water was done she put rose petals on top of the foam. She got into the tub, reflecting about her day. She was hot and horny all over again. She started to play with her already hard tits. Her pussy was screaming in protest and needing release. She closed her eyes, trying to imagine being fucked by the utility worker, Brad, Patty, Cynthia, and Joe. Each one of them servicing her. Licking and fucking her somehow. The imagery in the warm scented tub, in the candlelight was too much. Finally, her hands followed the all too well known path to her insatiable hot cunt. She needed to come again. She just had to have more!

Her fingers found her wet quivering pussy lips. She couldn't wait to build up, or for a lot of foreplay. She put her fingers in her twat, and rubbed her clit, until the bathroom vibrated with her screams. Her orgasmic screams. She cried out... Over and over again.... Each orgasm more intense than the next. Finally spent, she laid there in the tub. She laid there for a while. Then she cleaned up, and got out.

She dried off, and went into her bedroom. She donned on the sexy leather bustier and black pump high heels. She took the leather flogger, and slapped it against her hands. The harsh feel of the tether felt good against her hands, and made her quiver with anticipation. She grabbed the jelly dong. She couldn't wait to give Brad the show of a lifetime.

Kathy sat on the couch, waiting from Brad and Cinderella to get home. Finally, a light went on in the dark apartment. She studied them. He was gentlemanly, taking off her coat, making her feel comfortable.

The girlfriend was the girl next door type. All sunshine and lollipops. Very demure and feminine. Which meant one thing:

BORING!

She had soft brown hair, and blue eyes. Even a creamy complexion with freckles. She could see why he found her sweet.

Chapter Twenty

She noticed that he start kissing her. Then he started to feel her up. She looked like she was breathing hard. He started to lead her over to the bedroom. However, without Marcey seeing him, he looked over at Kathy's window.

"Wow!." he thought. She looks incredible!. He couldn't get over how Kathy looked sexy in or out of clothes. Look at that tight teddy. Her tits bulging out. Her long legs... She smiled boldly at him, knowing that he was turned on.

Kathy's gaze followed them to the bedroom. He gently undressed Marcey. Kissing her deeply. They embraced. His hands running up and down her back. Then his hands cupped her ass, bringing her more deeply into his embrace. Finally, he lay her on the bed, and stood up, slowly giving Marcey, and Kathy something to see. Kathy stood up, and slowly started to strip. She was able to get his gaze. First she lowered her straps slowly, then she ran her hands over her covered tits. She then ran her hand up and down the length of her sides. Her pussy ached again. She could see he was getting hard. She boldly looked at him and licked her lips. He knew he had to give Marcey some attention so she wouldn't get suspicious. But he just wanted to keep looking at Kathy.

He covered Marcey with the length of his body, nuzzling her neck, and then kissing her down to her creamy white breasts. She arched back and he sucked her tits. He then wondered what Kathy was doing. So he nudged Marcey's leg's open and knelt in between them. This would give him a good view of both women.

By this time, Kathy was totally undressed. Still looking at Brad, as if they were picking up where they left off. She was totally hot... She started to play with her tits. She rubbed and rubbed her tits. He rubbed Marcey's tits. She then rubbed them between her fingers and her thumbs. He did the same. Marecy cried out in surprise and pleasure. Brad had never done this to her before. Kathy then took the jelly dong and started to fuck her tits with it. Brad, totally blown away, began to fuck Marcey's titties with his own cock.

Marcey was very turned on. She cried out. It felt so good having Brad do this to her. He was full of surprises...

Kathy then took her hand, and began to play with her twat. She rubbed her wet pussy working her clit, as hard as she could. He cried out, coming over and over again. Brad put Marcey's hand on her pussy, and with his hand on top, made her come. She cried out over and over again. She felt so bad, yet the feeling was so good. Never had she let loose with him like this or any other man.

While he was kissing Marcey, Kathy took one of the roses and rubbed it all over herself. Brad looked over.... She is so totally hot. He wished he were that rose... rubbing himself all over her.

Taking her hand, she ran it over her wet pussy. She looked Brad right in his face, and licked, and sucked each finger. He took Marcey's hand, and rubbed her wet pussy with it. Then he stuck her fingers in his mouth, and then kissed her, so that she could taste herself. She then arched forward with one hand on the highboy, and started to spank herself with the flogger. It felt so good. Her juices were running down her thighs. *Whack! Whack! Whack!*

Kathy liked being in control. In control of not only her orgasm, but of Brad's and his unsuspecting girlfriend. *"She should actually thank me. She's going to get a fucking like she'll never get again."*

Kathy then took the jelly dong, at sat on the couch. She opened up her wet pussy for Brad. Then she let him watch her fuck herself over and over again with it. He finally fucked Marcey, with images of Kathy. He thrusted in and out of her over and over again. Marcey screamed each time. Brad finally pulled out of her, coming on her sweet belly.

Everyone lay spent. Finally, Brad looked over, only to find Kathy's apartment lights out. He wanted to say goodnight, but new he couldn't. He turned off the lights, and covered him and Marcey.

Chapter Twenty-One

Kathy woke up the next morning. She lay in bed trying to sort it all out. She knew that today was the day, she had patiently waited for.... The day when she would put those photos under snitty shitty Cynthia's door. The poor soul hasn't figured it out yet. She's probably wondering how she got under her sheets, naked. Surprised she hasn't been over to find out... But she will. Again... Patience....

Kathy got up, showered, dressed. She grabbed a quick glass of juice. She happened to look over at Brad's window... Uh-oh... Seems to be trouble in paradise.

From what she could see, each one of them looked pretty mad, and unhappy. Brad had his hands folded across his chest, and Marcey arms were flailing as if to prove a point. Finally, Marcey, in tears and anger stormed out of the apartment. Brad just kind of stood there. Then he sat down on his couch, with his head resting in his hands. He was there for quite some time. Then he looked at his watch, got up and left. "I would have loved to have been a fly on the wall for all of that." said Kathy aloud. She grabbed the envelope addressed to Cynthia, and left herself.

Kathy left her building to walk across the street to Cynthia's building. She went up on the elevator to the third floor. Sure that Cynthia, Ms. Dilligence, was at work by now, she knew it would be safe to leave the envelope under the door.

With that errand done, she got out her cell phone, and called Patty.
"Hello," answered Patty.
"Hi, it's me. What's up?"
"Nothing much. How about you?"
"It's all good. Do you have time for lunch or coffee today?"
"Sure. Cafe au Lait, and what time?"
"One thirty-ish?"
"Great. See you then."

Kathy decided to go clothes shopping. "*Brad was pretty upset. Maybe as a good neighbor I should take a bottle of wine over and comfort him?*" she thought. The more she thought about it, the more she smiled. She smiled like a Cheshire cat.

She entered the store. "*Let's see.... Something revealing, but not something too obvious... Something nice, but not too sweet. I don't want to look like a librarian or.... oh don't even think it... Cynthia.... God I would love to make her over....She would really be something... *"

Eventually, she did find exactly what she was looking. A dark purple sundress. It had a long v-neck, was sleeveless, and short. Now with black stockings for a garter belt, it will be perfect. She made the purchase.

She then went to the liquor store. She debated over what to buy. She kind of saw Brad as a red wine drinker. Yes, that sounds good. Okay... done...

Now, off to see Patty at Cafe au Lait.

It was crowded at the coffee shop, but Patty had arrived early and gotten a table.
"Hi."
"Hey."
"What's going on?" asked Kathy.
Patty started to tell her about her photo shoot. It was shooting models for a spring catalog. It paid well, and she would be traveling to Europe.
"That's great!" said Kathy. "I am so thrilled for you."

"Thanks. So what's going on in your little worlds?"

"Well, I put the photographs under Cynthia's door this morning. I figure she'll need the evening to get over it. As for Brad, well.... he watched me, and I watched him doing his 'girlfriend.' But this morning, they had some kind of fight, because she was in tears, and left in a big huff and puff."

"So, what's the plan."

"Glad you asked. I think he'll need a little comforting. So I bought this dress and a bottle of wine. If he won't come to my place, I'll go to his. But I'm hoping that he'll come to my place so that I can kill two birds with one stone."

"How's that?" Patty asked.

"When Cynthia gets that envelope, she's going to want to speak with me. What I'm hoping is that she sees me with Brad. Either way, I'm going to do him... So I still get what I want in the end."

"Do you like this guy?" asked Patty.

"I like him, but not the way you think. I think he's a nice guy, but I just want to do him. That's it. Besides, I'm hoping that he'll find someone else who will really fulfill him instead of Cinderella. She seemed boring to me."

"Aren't you the do-gooder?" joked Patty.

"Well, that's just the way I am," Kathy said back jokingly.

The both had a good laugh. Eventually, they parted ways, and Kathy headed back to the apartment.

Chapter Twenty-Two

Cynthia was just coming in the lobby from work. It had been a very tedious day. All the correspondences had to be gotten out. All the faxing. The temporary staff that didn't do things correctly... Just a day of cleaning up after people's incompetence...

But, finally home, and looking forward to changing out of her clothes, and putting on a dressing gown. She would listen to some Mozart and Chopin, with a nice cup of Earl Grey tea.

She got off the elevator, found her key, and entered her apartment. She found a big envelope under her door. "What in the world could this be? Why would anyone do something like this?" she said aloud.

She picked up the envelope, put it and her keys down on the coffee table. She went and hung up her clothes, showered, and changed into her floor length dressing gown with robe and slippers. She had the tea pot on the stove boiling. As it was just beginning to whistle, she had put the tea leaves in the pot. At least tea didn't make her ill. That stuff Ms. Dexter brought over the other day, while good stuff, had a very strange effect on her. She just wish she could remember what happened.

Nothing was stolen. Everything looked in tact. Cynthia just couldn't understand why she had a headache, and why she was undressed in bed. Plus, all of her garments scattered over the floor. The least someone could have done was pick them up.

At any rate, she fixed her tea with a slice of lemon and one lump of sugar. She brought the cup and saucer out to the living room, and then began to play her classical music.

Ah... The beautiful work of the great composers... The rhythm and use of instruments was exciting. A sound truly to behold. She just sit back and let the stress of the day melt away. She then opened her eyes after a while. Cynthia picked up the envelope and opened it. She read the note:

Dear Cynthia,

Just a remembrance of our afternoon together. Hope we can do it again soon. Hope you enjoyed this afternoon as much as I did.

Kathy

"Remembrance? Do it again soon?" thought Cynthia.

She then started to rifle through the photos. "Oh my God!" screamed Cynthia. She couldn't believe the photos! Her and Ms. Dexter! It couldn't be. How could this have happened, and me being there and not knowing it?

Surely, she would have stopped the whole disgusting affair. Dear God... What if she has negatives? Who took the photos? She had a lot of questions, and no answers.

She went to the window to see if Ms. Dexter was home. She was home alright, but she was entertaining. So far with clothes on....

"We will see about this tomorrow."

However, the longer she looked out her window, the more she slowly started to see.

Chapter Twenty-Three

Kathy was waiting for Brad to come home from work. She watched him enter his apartment. Damn he was fine. Those pants really hugged his ass well.

She was already showered and dressed in her outfit. He came out to the balcony, and looked out at the evening. As she knew would happen, he looked in her direction. She smiled warmly, and waved. He gave her half a smile, and a small wave. She motioned for him to pick up the phone, and so he did.

"Hello." said Kathy.

"Hi."

"So, how are you?" asked Kathy.

"I've been better?"

"Sorry to hear that. What's going on?"

"I don't want to bother you with my problems."

"Hey, I asked didn't I? What's going on?"

"Look, I can see your expecting someone. I don't want to intrude."

"Actually, I was hoping to expect you."

"What?" Brad asked.

"Look. I don't mean to be in your business, but I kind of saw that things weren't good between you and your girlfriend this morning. I thought you might need someone to talk to."

"Actually, ex-girlfriend."

"Ooh... Sorry."

"Actually, maybe it's for the best... I mean, I liked her, but there always seemed like there was something missing..."

"I think I understand," offered a 'sympathetic' Kathy. "Look, come on over. No use sitting around by yourself. I have this great wine here, and we can just talk. Besides, it's Friday night, the weekend is here, and if you get a little buzzed, who cares? Right?"

"Okay, what's your apartment number?"

"525."

"Be over in a few minutes."

Chapter Twenty-Five

There was a knock at the door. Kathy opened the door, and there was Brad.

"Hello. Come on in."

"Thanks."

"Sit down. Relax. Here, have some wine."

Brad excepted the wine.

"So," probed Kathy, "What happened?"

"She didn't like the way I treated her."

"What?"

"Yeah, she said she felt like a trollop."

"Brad, I watched... She enjoyed herself. The problem wasn't you. And, she's wrong to leave you with the blame. The problem is her... She's not being honest with herself or you. She's not in touch with her sexuality. You brought out feelings that she's probably had, but just isn't honest enough to deal with."

Brad took that all in... He always suspected something like that about Marcey. Like she was just to goody good to believe. What's wrong with wanting a little more in the romance department?

As if she read his mind, Kathy went on to say, "You know, if people would just be more open and honest. If women would stop expecting a man to know what she wants, and just tell him, things between men and women would be totally different. Too many games, drama, bullshit... Just keep it real."

"I wish more women were like you."

"Thank you."

"No, Kathy, seriously. If you want it harder, I'll do it harder. If you want slower, I'll do it slower. But hell, I can't read people's minds."

"You shouldn't have to," said Kathy. "A relationship is a two-way street."

"Cheers."

"Cheers."

They clinked glasses. There was a lot more clinking, and a lot more toasts. Soon both of them were pretty well 'toasted.'

"I'm glad you talked me into coming over, Kathy."

"I'm glad you did, too."

"You know," said Brad, "I have a confession to make."
"What's that?"

"Well," Brad continued, "When I was with Marcey last night, I just wanted to keep looking over here at you." "Did you now?" purred Kathy. "Yeah," admitted Brad.

Slowly, he reached for her. They began to kiss. He really had been wanting this from the first time he watched her get off. He couldn't believe that this could actually be happening. She moved in more towards him. Their tongues swirled. He reached for her and began to feel her up. The weight of her titty felt so good. He was like a kid who wanted to unwrap a Christmas gift – just tear off the paper.

He began to kiss down her neck... Damn she smelled good. He kissed down to the open v-neck that revealed her cleavage. She sighed and tilted her head back. He started to lower the zipper slowly, little by little. Finally, he was able to set her titties free.

He stood back and looked at her. Her hard pouting tits just teasing him to suck on them. He looked at her; her smoldering eyes, urging him on. He took one in his mouth. She gasped. He played with her other bared nipple.

"Oh baby, it feels so good. Make my titties hard."
He licked, and licked. He massaged, and rubbed. Finally doing both titties at the same time.

"My pussy is so wet for you."
He wanted to find out. He unzipped the dress the rest of the way. He saw her black lace garter belt, no panties, with just stockings. He rubbed her bare twat with his hand. She shivered with delight.

He wanted to make her wait... Make her suffer... Make her want it for all the times he watched her....For all the hard-ons and cold showers. But most of all, he wanted, at least for tonight to get back at Marcey and be with a real woman. A woman who wasn't afraid of getting what she wants. A woman who gave pleasure as much as she took pleasure. An equality; not a man having to do all the work; all the planning; all the thinking; all the guessing... Just two people keeping it real...

She was sexy... Curvaceous body... nice set of titties, and a pussy dying to be fucked.... But it was her... Her energy... her candidness... Her.

He plunged his fingers into her wet pouting pussy. She was so wet... Her slit was so slick. He fucked her in and out with his fingers. She screamed in no time. Finally she screamed, "Eat me Brad! Eat my pussy.!.. If I don't come I'll explode! " He got off the couch, and crouched down in front of her... He then spread her stocking legs apart as far as he could. He opened her pretty, wet, silky pussy lips. She shuddered. He then went down on her.

At first, he just went lightly up and down her slit. She thought she would die if he didn't eat her soon. She moaned, "Ahh..." She twisted and turned, grabbing onto the couch for strength. She thought she would go through the roof. A sweet torture...

Then he started to lick further and further into her wet wanting twat. She shook from side to side. She reached for his hair. She was rifling his hair back and forth. Then wanting him to bring her off, she clamped his head down into her cunt. She held him prisoner, to bring her off.

His tongue found her clit. She screamed again. "Ohh... Ohh... Yeah baby... Eat me! Don't stop! It feels so fucking good! Aah!!!"

He made her come over and over again. Most women would have been exhausted. But not her. All the climaxing made her like a lioness, wanting more, and wanting to give back just as much in return.

He got back up on the couch with her. They kissed, and she stole back her taste from him. Then she stood up, stepped out of the dress, and threw it to the side like a used rag.

While she would have loved to have taken off his shirt, she just had to have him now. She wanted to blow him; fuck him... but most importantly, she wanted to come again while riding his cock. She would fuck him for everything it was worth. She wanted to bring them both off, screaming the roof down.

First, she licked his cock... She really had to restrain herself, because she really wanted to blow him. She pretended to be licking an icecream cone. Lick, swirl, lick, swirl... She loved blowing guys... She liked having them right where she wanted them. To have them literally at her mercy... under her power... That was sexy as hell, too.

He laid back, not believing what was happening. Not caring too much either. This was just for the moment. But it was so damn good. He held her head down too. Give her a little taste of her own medicine. Literally, and ha, ha, figuratively. She really was pumping his cock now. Up and down, up and down... She then started to slow down... Kathy then eyed him, and spanked his erect cock on her tongue. Her boldness; her intensity... It made him even more hard.

She might make him come in her mouth later on. But for now, she had to, no.. she must ride that cock now. She sat on his cock, and bounced up and down on it. Her tits were jiggling everywhere. The feeling was unbelievable. He grabbed hold of her ass, and found a way to kiss her.

After a while she stopped. She laid back on the coffee table, and put her legs up in the air. He put them over his shoulder. He ran his hands up and down her silk stocking legs, with her come-fuck-me pumps on. He drilled her wet hole in and out, in and out. She screamed every time his cock touched her clit. She reached down to play with herself, as he fucked her. She rubbed her clit, and screamed. She was so hot. Not afraid to go after what she wanted. And right now, that was to come at all costs!

Then he took her legs, and did what he always wanted to do – he put her legs, stockings and pumps and bent them back over her stomach, reaching over her shoulders. He got the whole view... her glistening bare pussy just begging to be fucked.

He re-inserted his cock, and fucked her as hard as he could. The orgasms were so intense, she screamed, "Oh my God!!" She came over and over again. He was sweating and grunting until he finally pulled out.

She knew he was about to come. She went over towards him, had him sit on the couch. She grabbed his cock and sucked in hard. She made her lips hard and taut around his cock, letting it slide back and forth on her wet tongue. He needed to get off... He pumped his cock into her mouth as hard as he could. The pressure of her sucking, her tongue, the sight of her sucking on him... His junk exploded in her mouth. She sucked down every creamy bit. She wanted it... All of it... She was determined to have all of him. He screamed his release.

She went back up on the couch. She let him lie there for a while. Then his eyes opened and they looked at each other.

"It's late. Why don't you stay over." she offered.
"Lead the way."
She took him into the bedroom. Typically, she didn't let men stay over, but he was loaded and tired. They both went to sleep.

Chapter Twenty-Six

They slept peacefully. Then morning came. He looked over to find himself in a strange bed, with a woman other than Marcey. Look at her... She looks so peaceful. Like an angel.... Then he had to remember last night, and what a vixen Kathy could be.

So as not to wake her, he crept softly out of the bed. He collected his clothes and went into the bathroom.

Although it wasn't as floral as some females' bathrooms, you could see signs of femininity. There were marble tiles, a sunken enclosed bathtub. Candles, potpourri, and a small floral arrangement in the corner of the vanity. Nothing overly feminine yet sophisticated feminine taste for sure. Definitely wasn't a guy's bathroom. Ha, ha...

He grabbed a towel, so it would be close by when he got out of the shower. He turned the taps of water on. He got in the shower, glad to have some time to himself to regroup. He ran his whole body under the shower. The pelting water felt good. Maybe he could wash off all the confusion... all the anger... all the nonsense...

He lathered up his whole torso from head to foot. He rinsed off. Then he toweled off, and put his clothes back on.

Kathy lay there. She knew he was up and about. She knew he had been staring at her. Typically, she didn't let guys stay over. But, he wasn't the same as other guys. He was just a nice guy, who just had his heart broken.

Typically, she would have went in the shower and surprised him. But, she knew he needed a little space. That's what was nice about being like her... She wasn't clingy or needy. Some women would have already been badgering him about what their status was, or were they now exclusive. That was the nice thing about no commitments. No promises to be broken, no breakups, no bullshit... Easy. Clean. Straight on the line.

He finally emerged from the bathroom. He saw that she was awake.

"Good Morning."
"Good Morning."
"Hope you don't mind, I grabbed a shower."
"No. Did you find everything you needed?"
"Yes. Thanks."

"If I were more of a cook, I would cook breakfast."

"Not to worry," he said. "I'll take you to breakfast."

"Great! I'll get up and get ready." said Kathy.

"Hey, while you're getting ready, I'll go to my apartment, and grab my wallet." said Brad.

"Okay. I'll meet you downstairs in about a half hour. Good?"

"Good."

Kathy got up and ready.

Chapter Twenty-Seven

She wore a white peasant blouse with a jean skirt, with bronze open-toe sandals. He was waiting for her downstairs in the lobby of her building. He changed, too. Very casual. Khaki pants, and a short-sleeved Polo shirt. He drove her to a delightful little place called Rose Garden Kitchen. "They have the best breakfast here. I don't know about you, but I'm starved!" said Brad. " I could eat." said Kathy.

The conversation during the drive and throughout breakfast had been light and casual. Finally, Brad said,

"... Look... about last night..."

"Brad, there's no problems here. It was what it was."

"You're sure."

"Definitely. I just hope that the next woman will be someone who you're really more in tune with. Someone who is just what you want and need. Not just someone to go through the motions with."

"You're really something. I appreciate you understanding. But can I ask you a question? "Asked Brad.

"Let me guess... How come no regular guy?"

"Yes," stammered Brad.

"Because I know what it's like to be hurt. So I like the lifestyle that I've chosen. Not that I can do it all my life, but for now... It's okay."

"That's honest enough," said Brad.

"No other way to be." said Kathy.

The trip back was filled with laughs and good conversation. If anything, she had made a friend.

Chapter Twenty-Eight

Kathy returned by noon to her apartment. What to do with the rest of the day? Just then, her question got answered by a ring of the intercom.

"Yes?"
"It's Cynthia Wentworth."
"Oh this should be good." Kathy thought.
"I'll buzz you int."
Within five minutes Cynthia was knocking at her door.

"Why hello Cynthia," greeted Kathy.
"May I come in?" asked Cynthia.
"Surely." Kathy stepped aside to allow Cynthia to enter. She noticed that Cynthia had the envelope of photos with her.

"Can I offer you something to drink?"
"I don't know that I would want that again." scoffed Cynthia.
"Please take a seat."
Cynthia sat on the sofa, as Kathy sat down opposite of her.

"I would like an explanation for *these*." Cynthia demanded.
"Are you asking me for an explanation, or demanding it of me?"
"I need answers to things that I don't remember participating in."
"Very well, " said Kathy. "What do you want to know?"
"What do I want to know?" Cynthia asked disbelievingly.
"I want to know about these!" Cynthia dumped the pictures over the coffee table.

"Look," Kathy started irritably, "You became ill, I helped you into the bedroom so you could lie down. One thing led to another, and we slept together. There... That's it in a nutshell."

"If we were both in the pictures, who took the pictures?" demanded Cynthia.

"Remember I had a friend, that I said would be dropping by, as that we had plans? The friend is a photographer, and she took them. She thought we were beautiful."

"Beautiful!" shrieked Cynthia, "This filth is beautiful!"
"Cynthia, it's not filth. It's being human. Try it sometimes!"

"How dare you!"
"Look, bitch, come off of your soap box. You're no better than any damn body else. As much as I feel sorry for you, that's how much I think you deserve the self-made hell that you live in."

"What do you mean by that? I have a wonderful fulfilled life."rebounded Cynthia.

"So does a corpse! I wouldn't want your life, if they paid me a million dollars for it. You're mean and miserable; you have no life; you look like a woman of sixty-two, when you can't be any more than thirty. Seriously, what the hell?"Kathy told her off.

"My life is none of your business," cried Cynthia.
"Neither is mine... How dare you judge me! Although you act like it, you're not my mother! You're just pissed off that I have the guts to be what you can't be. You're in a little cocoon too afraid of your own damn shadow! You've got a wall built up all around you! Well how's that working for you?!" Kathy insulted her.

"Well... I never..."

"Maybe you should try it!"

"I don't have to behave like some side show trollop!" shot back Cynthia. *Slap!* Kathy slapped Cynthia across the face. She had just had enough of this provoking woman!

Cynthia held her struck face. The anger boiled up inside her... She could feel the blood pounding in her veins! She came across at Kathy with even a vigor that she didn't know that she possessed. She was on top of Kathy swinging and flailing her arms with all her might.

Kathy was surprised, yet totally fed up.

"Bitch!" *Punch!*
"Tramp!" *Slap!*
"Ice Princess! *Slug!*
"Whore!" *Pound!*

"*Whore!*" Kathy swore, "*You frigid little cunt*!" Kathy reached over and ripped the pearl buttons off of Cynthia's blouse.

"You're going to replace that!" screamed Cynthia. "Don't worry, my grandma has one just like it. You can have hers!"offered Kathy.

Cynthia got so mad that she gave Kathy the same treatment. She tore open Kathy's blouse, and out came Kathy's tits.

Kathy lunged on top of Cynthia. Now both women were on the floor. What started out as a heated discussion was turning into a cat fight, with both women on top of each other rolling all over the floor.

As the fight continued, Kathy tore open Cynthia's blouse all the way. She was even so mad she ripped the sleeves off of her as well. Kathy was on top of Cynthia, and had her arms pinned down. Cynthia rocked from side to side screaming. Kathy tugged at the side zipper in Cynthia's skirt.

Finally, Kathy got up. "Get up bitch!"
Cynthia got up, but when she did, the skirt fell down the length of her.

Kathy still mad as hell, came at her and pinned her to a wall. Both were still struggling against each other and the wall and the wall. With one free hand, Cynthia slapped Kathy across the face, just like she had done to her.

"You little cunt! Now you're going to get it!"

Kathy reached for the front hook on Cynthia's bra. She roughly yanked hard on it enough for it to open up. Cynthia's small breasts spilled out of the bra.

Realizing that she was too exposed, Cynthia tried to cover herself, but Kathy came at her again. She had her pinned to the wall, with her hands pinned down above her head.

They were face-to -face, nose-to-nose, titty-to-titty.

Each one looked menacingly into each others eyes. Hate, anger, contempt... each looked into the others eyes with these emotions. Time stood still...

Finally, through whatever, their lips met, tongues swirled. Kathy grasped Cynthia's face with both hands. They kissed with as much gusto as they had when they were fighting. Kathy began to start kissing down the length of Cynthia's neck. She turned her head and gasped at how good Kathy's kisses were. Slowly, Kathy made her way down to Cynthia's exposed titties. She couldn't control herself any longer. Kathy pushed the tits together, and starting sucking on them as hard as she could. "Ohh!" Cynthia exhaled out. She was breathing heavily. Kathy's sucking felt so good. She never knew it could feel so good. It was just like when she watched Kathy last night with that man. The way he licked and sucked her breasts. She was feeling the same way he made Kathy feel.

Cynthia, started to stroke Kathy's hair. Kathy slid down the length of Cynthia's torso. She kept her hands on Cynthia's tits; rubbing, and playing with them. It was a sweet torture, that was going to get a lot hotter, steamier, and creamier...

Kathy needed both hands to tug down Cynthia's pantyhose. Once free, Kathy's hand went back up to play with a titty. She then found Cynthia's slit. She slid her tongue into that hot sweet spot. She lightly licked it up and down sending shivers of delight through Cynthia. Cynthia by now was gasping and panting. Holding onto the wall for dear life. Then, Kathy's tongue found her clit. Cynthia could be contained no more. She screamed for dear life, "Ohhhh!!! Ahhh!!!" "You like that? You like coming for me, baby?" teased Kathy. "That's it baby, come for me some more!" Cynthia came over and over again. She stood naked against a wall, having a woman suck her tits, and eat her pussy. It was as if she turned into a new person, and that the old Cynthia no longer existed.

When her tongue grew tired, Kathy replaced it with her free hand. She was far from done with Cynthia yet. She felt as if she were breathing life into her, and wasn't giving up yet.

"That's it, baby... Be a good girl and come for me some more." Kathy teased. "You like that don't you Cindy? You like it when I make you come, don't you?" She rubbed her clit harder and harder. Cynthia came again and again.

Kathy slid back up to Cynthia, still rubbing her clit. She purred in her ear, "Tell me Cindy... Tell me... Tell me you like it when I make you come."Cynthia didn't answer at first . So Kathy rubbed her clit harder and faster. Cynthia thought she would faint. "Tell me,"Kathy growled in her ear. "Yes!" screamed Cynthia. "Yes, what?"demanded Kathy in a low whispering voice. Cynthia could feel Kathy's hot breath in her ear. Kathy worked her tender bud again, but with even more force and speed. *"I like it when you make me come!"* screamed Cynthia. She climaxed once more, and then slowly took her finger out of Cynthia's soaked pussy. She smeared her finger over Cynthia's lips, then taking the taste back with a long lingering kiss.

Kathy led Cynthia into her bedroom. She lie Cynthia down on her satin bedspread. Kathy stripped the rest of her clothes off, and laid down next to her.

She kissed Cynthia some more. Then she placed Cynthia's hand on her titty. Cynthia looked shy for a second. "Rub my titty, just the way I rubbed yours." Cynthia was a little shy at first. So, Kathy put her hand over Cynthia's.

She did this with both of Cynthia's hands. Kathy's head began to roll back and forth across the pillow. "Yeah Cindy... Yeah, that's real good. You're making me so wet, and my titties real hard. Ummm."

After a while, she left one of her hands on her tits, and slowly slid Cynthia's hand down her body. Slowly, lingering... Until finally, it came to her shaved mound. She took Cynthia's fingers and glided them up and down her wet slit. She lifted Cynthia's fingers to her mouth, and sucked Cynthia's fingers. Then she replaced the hand back into her soaked pussy, and kissed Cynthia hard and long. She helped Cynthia find her clit, and held her hand there, and worked her hand back and forth, until Cynthia got the feeling for it. Then she let Cynthia on her own to bring her off. "Yeah... Yeah, baby... Harder, Good, So good..... Oh!!!, Oh!!!Ahh!!!!!." She screamed as Cynthia made her come over and over.

Cynthia liked that she could have some power over Kathy. She liked knowing that she could give the other woman pleasure. She liked hearing her scream.

They lay there for the longest time. Kathy stroked Cynthia's arm, back and forth.

"I never knew..." Cynthia started, but never finished.
"It's the start of a new life for you."
"But now what?" asked Cynthia.

Chapter Twenty-Nine

Joe, the baker, lived across the street. He knew of Kathy for a long time. He knew some day he would fuck her. That day at the shop, he would always remember.

He had been video taping Kathy for some time. She never disappointed him. At least once a week, he video taped her. Whether playing with herself or someone else. He didn't much care.

He made friends of the college kids that had a view of her bedroom. He set them up with the video equipment and everything. He gave them so much money. Then, he put the tapes together, and sold them to a Ms. Chen. She was an older woman, who ran some kind of sex mansion for get aways for the spoiled rich. But she also sold videos overseas. So the people in the videos would never know, because it would never be seen here in the states. He made a lot of money so far. After all, how could he live in a luxury penthouse apartment on a baker's salary? He called over to Ray, "Hey Ray, make sure you get her in the bedroom. Her and some other broad are going at it." "Yeah, Joe, I've got them. Wow! You should see them going at each other." "I know," said Joe, "They started in her living room, and ended up in the bedroom."

"I'll have this over to you tomorrow, Joe."
"Thanks. I have to get some sleep. I have to be on night turn tonight to do donuts and breads."

He, he, he... That's right baby... I'm the Baker Man....

Epilogue

Well, let's see....

Brad, started to go to wild night clubs, strip clubs and the like. For a while, he became a real playboy. But, he finally found a girl that he married. Oh, did I mention that he got out of the credit card processing business and bought a strip club.? Yeah, he married one of the strippers.... So he finally got a hot woman.

Cynthia, was a changed woman. Who knew that some orgasms could really change a person? She gave all her old lady clothes to the poor, and went shopping. Kathy helped her pick out some new outfits, a new hairdo, and some makeup. What a total transformation! She's much freer and happier. She found a nice man, who encourages her to be herself. The true Cynthia finally came out... Oh, my bad... She now likes to be called Cindy....

Patty, came back from Europe. She now does video productions services as well as photography. She recently married a nice woman. Kathy was the maid of honor.

The lineman, after fucking Kathy, finally got his confidence back. He met a nice girl, they got married, and he couldn't be happier, with a baby on the way. So things do work out for a reason...

As for Kathy, she only led her "adventure," for a little bit longer. About a year and a half later, one of the guys that she laid, she really came to like and have feelings for. They're planning their wedding for August. It will be a destination wedding at the beach. She definitely will not be wearing white...Too traditional... Not her style. Some things never change...

Then, Joe, the Baker Man...
The old sleaze bag is still banging women, and filming porno for money. But, he got so much money from the filming that he bought the Stover Bake Shop, and turned it into a bakery/coffee shop/diner. It's now called, "Joe's Place."

The End.

Fruit Punch
16 oz. unsweetened Pineapple Juice
16 oz. cranberry-raspberry juice
1 tsp. sweetened lime juice
16 oz. lemon-lime soda
¼ c. light rum

Mix ingredients together. Pour over ice. Drink responsibly.